SKILLS IN COUNSELING WOMEN

SKILLS IN COUNSELING WOMEN

The Feminist Approach

By

MARY NOMME RUSSELL, Ph.D.

School of Social Work
University of British Columbia
Vancouver, British Columbia, Canada

CHARLES C THOMAS • PUBLISHER
Springfield • Illinois • U.S.A.

Published and Distributed Throughout the World by

CHARLES C THOMAS • PUBLISHER
2600 South First Street
Springfield, Illinois 62717

©*1984 by* CHARLES C THOMAS • PUBLISHER

ISBN 0-398-04971-8

Library of Congress Catalog Card Number: 83-18201

With THOMAS BOOKS *careful attention is given to all details of manufacturing and
design. It is the Publisher's desire to present books that are satisfactory as to their physical
qualities and artistic possibilities and appropriate for their particular use.* THOMAS
BOOKS *will be true to those laws of quality that assure a good name and good will.*

Printed in the United States of America

SC-R-3

Library of Congress Cataloging in Publication Data

Russell, Mary Nomme.
    Skills in counseling women.

    Bibliography: p.
    Includes index.
    1. Feminist therapy.   2. Women—Counseling of.
I. Title.
RC489.F45R87   1984   158.3   83-18201
ISBN 0-398-04971-8

To Julia and Jason,
to whom the future belongs

PREFACE

The goal of this book is to provide counselors and counseling students with a specific and concrete explanation of feminist counseling. To this end, counseling practice is analyzed here and broken down into components or skills relevant from a feminist perspective, and each skill is discussed in turn. Theoretical foundations, empirical evidence, and clinical examples are presented for each skill. Role-playing exercises are also provided for each skill, with accompanying counseling transcripts of role enactment by experienced feminist counselors. The prescribed format of didactic learning, role playing, exposure to modeling, and remedial role playing is encouraged for mastery of each skill.

This study, then, takes a microcounseling approach to the teaching of individual skills. This approach has demonstrated its effectiveness in skill acquisition and hence is deemed ideally suitable for the approach to feminist counseling presented in this book.

Since feminist counseling is a new and developing counseling philosophy, experienced counselors as well as novice counselors can benefit from skill acquisition. Most counselors will ultimately be dealing primarily with female clients, for women are the primary consumers of counseling services. The counseling approach required in that context is one that specifically meets the needs and concerns of contemporary women, and that is the approach provided by feminist counseling.

This book applies feminist counseling skills to a wide range of women seeking counseling services. To date, descriptions of feminist counseling in the literature have been limited to clients who were young and radical. Such clients identified themselves with feminism and sought out feminist counseling services. This book is different from those earlier studies in demonstrating that the skills of feminist counseling are applicable to the general population of women who seek counseling. The clinical examples described here include older women, even conservative women with no feminist identification, who sought help from traditional counseling sources. Feminist counseling skills were found to be equally beneficial to all.

To validate any given counseling approach, it is necessary to demonstrate a cohesive theoretical framework, a clearly definable array of clinical skills, and empirical evidence of the effectiveness of the approach. To this end, this book offers a tripartite approach to each skill, an approach grounded in theory, research, and practice. Although not all dimensions of feminist counseling find equal support in each of these areas, sufficient support is available to validate each skill presented here and thus, in general, to validate feminist counseling as a discipline.

Finally, each feminist counseling skill is not only identified here but also measured by developing a corresponding scale. The scales are presented in the hope that they will be used both by counselors in evaluating their own performance and by researchers in future investigations and evaluations of the feminist counseling approach. It is hoped that counselors as well as researchers will use the methodology offered in this book to further validation efforts of feminist counseling skills singly and in combination. It is through such validation in the field that we shall be able to demonstrate that feminist counseling is indeed a viable and effective approach to the problems of contemporary women.

ACKNOWLEDGMENTS

This book represents the culmination of several years of clinical experience, study, and teaching. Numerous individuals and several institutions made it all possible.

To the Psychology Department at Simon Fraser University I am grateful for the opportunity to pursue my interest in feminist counseling in an academic context. In particular I appreciate the support of my advisors, Ronald Roesch, Meredith Kimball, and Ray Koopman, who encouraged an empirical approach to this area.

To the School of Social Work at the University of British Columbia I am grateful for the opportunity to develop and experiment with this approach to teaching feminist counseling skills.

I am grateful to Tirthankar Bose of U.B.C. for his help with the manuscript.

Two feminist counselors were generous with their time and in sharing their counseling experiences with me. Some of their work is presented in the clinical examples. I gratefully acknowledge my debt to Margaret Penn and Julie Brickman.

And finally, I would like to thank the many unnamed clients, students, and colleagues who shared their experiences with me, who challenged and sharpened my thinking, and who demonstrated that women sharing experiences collectively can formulate a new understanding and a new perception of women today.

CONTENTS

Contents

SKILLS IN COUNSELING WOMEN

Chapter 1

INTRODUCTION

OVERVIEW

Feminist counseling is counseling of women by women for women. It is counseling of women because female social situations and developmental issues are specifically incorporated into the counseling process. It is by women inasmuch as female counselors potentially can achieve a more thorough understanding of the female condition. And it is for women because it aims to redress the gender-based inequities that contribute to clients' distress.

Feminist counseling is now recognized by professional counselors as the choice counseling approach for female clients (Collins, 1982; Gilbert, 1980; Rawlings & Carter, 1977; Sturdivant, 1980). Traditional counseling approaches, developed and used in the past, are increasingly being subjected to scrutiny and found lacking in a positive orientation to women, riddled with sex role stereotypes, and providing little support for the total development of female clients.

This increased endorsement of feminist counseling, however, has not been reinforced by either a clear specification of what constitutes feminist counseling or a detailed description of the distinctive aspects of feminist clinical practice. To the contrary, it has been suggested that feminist counseling consists not of distinctive skills or methods but rather of traditional counseling methods purged of sexism or presented by a counselor with a feminist perspective or philosophy (Collins, 1982; Sturdivant, 1980). Clearly, such views ignore the nature of actual feminist clinical practice, which is unique and distinguishable from more traditional counseling approaches.

This book proposes that feminist counseling be viewed as a distinctive counseling method that has grown out of a nucleus of discrete and specifiable counseling skills. While some of these skills are also common to other counseling approaches, their purpose and use are different in feminist counseling. Furthermore, it is the constellation and interaction of the skills in the clinical encounter that define feminist counseling, rather than any individual skill in isolation.

The present delineation of feminist counseling skills and the recommended mode for learning such skills are based on Ivey's (1971) microcounseling model. This model prescribes that the totality of counseling practice be broken down into specific skills and that each be presented singly. Each skill to be mastered then needs to be cognitively assimilated and rehearsed in role playing. This role playing must be monitored against the skill demonstration of an experienced counselor so that discrepancies can be noted. Modifications and refinements of skill performance can then be made based upon personal observation as well as the suggestions of a supportive supervisor. These changes can subsequently be incorporated into remedial role playing. This sequence of theoretical learning, rehearsal, modeling, and remedial practice is considered optimal for acquiring counseling skills. While implementation of every aspect of the sequence may not always be feasible or even necessary, a generally close approximation of the sequence is recommended.

Having mastered the central skills of feminist counseling separately, the counselor is ready to integrate them into the clinical encounter. This integration of feminist counseling skills with other basic counseling skills within the individual counselor's style and their apposite application at appropriate times are what produces effective feminist counseling practice.

THE DEVELOPMENT OF FEMINIST COUNSELING

Feminist counseling is a recent innovation in the century-long history of psychotherapy and professional counseling practice. Previous counseling theories and practices had been based on a social perspective in which males were seen to predominate and women to exist as appendages, auxiliaries, and supports. Women's identity and development were not seen to have an independent value or existence. This perspective prevailed in counseling despite the fact that women were the primary recipients of counseling services.

Women more than men have consistently sought and used counseling services to alleviate their psychological distress (Gove, 1979; Levine, Kamin & Levine, 1974). Counselors and therapists have recognized and accepted this discrepancy as the norm, as another manifestation of the essential difference between the sexes.

Women's greater need for psychological help has generally been attributed by counselors to some inherent weakness in their physical or psychological makeup. Early psychological theories suggested that women's anatomy, which was considered to be a deficient version of male anatomy, predisposed them to inadequate psychological development manifested in weak willpower and moral judgment. Women were considered to be constitutionally unable to reach the same levels of psychological maturity as men. In conjunction with this anatomical focus, early psychological theories attributed hysterical reactions in women to the phenomenon of the wandering womb (Bart & Scully, 1979). The supposed instability of women's reproductive organs was in part held responsible for their proclivity to psychological distress. It is ironic that in the one area where women clearly attain something impossible for men, namely, bearing children, a fundamental weakness or fault was posited.

Today, views of women's anatomy, physiology, and psychology are more sophisticated, but unfortunately the theme of inherent female inferiority persists. Much attention has been paid to female sex hormones, which are said to have an unsettling impact on women's psychological equilibrium. Women are frequently taken to be at the mercy of their raging hormones, which make them unfit for sustained heavy responsibilities or commitments (Parlee, 1973). Strangely enough, the corresponding male sex hormones are said to have innumerable beneficial qualities. Male sex hormones make men strong, assertive, and brave. Female sex hormones make women irrational, irritable, labile, and incompetent. Again it is a strange perception that women, who have the primary responsibility for bearing and rearing children, for perpetuating the species and socializing future generations, should biologically and psychologically be so feebly equipped to do so.

Recent theories of cognition and perception have also posited sex differences that reinforce the view of woman as being less effective. Although it has been demonstrated that women's brains are not smaller than men's brains (as once was thought) and may indeed be slightly larger, current theory suggests that women use the wrong half! Or, in terms of perception, it is suggested that women's lesser capacity for visual-spatial perception makes them inherently and increasingly inept in this mechanistic and technological society. It seems not to matter what area of the anatomy or psyche is being investigated for sex differences; the results tend to be the same. Psychological theories indicate that women are clearly different from men, and the difference is always unfavorable to women.

Given this theoretical background, it is not surprising that counselors have striven only to bolster the functioning of their female clients or to raise it to minimally acceptable levels. If women are constitutionally inferior, it follows that counseling should direct them into limited channels, into predestined and prescribed lesser places. Counseling for women, given this perspective, has provided only limited opportunities for growth, conflict resolution, and personal development. The counseling process for women has consisted of a progressive reconciliation with or adjustment to their bounded role and status. Counseling did not, as it often did for men, lead to an exciting and exhilarating testing, exploring, and expanding of personal limits. Women who did question and rebel against the structures of socially prescribed notions of femininity and womanhood were generally not supported by their counselors. In fact, the counselors of these rebellious women were frequently the first to label the women as sick or deviant (Abramowitz, Abramowitz, Jackson & Gomes, 1973).

Understandably, a time came when the results of counseling based on these theories became unsatisfactory to most female clients. Women's growing dissatisfaction with the results of such counseling led to criticism of both the underlying theories and the prevailing clinical practices.

Chesler (1970) was one of the early critics of the institution of psychotherapy, which she claimed was second only to marriage in its control and suppression of women. This theme of counseling serving to control women rather than to aid them has been reiterated by numerous critics of traditional counseling practice (Hurvitz, 1973; Simon, 1970; Tennov, 1976). The expression *cooling the mark* came to denote the counseling objective of defusing women's anger without changing or even addressing the inequities that generated the anger in the first place (Lipman-Blumen, 1972).

Not only did these critics say that traditional counseling was controlling women, they also argued that it was oppressing women and that others were benefiting from this oppression. As long as women were successfully socialized into a predominately nurturing, supportive, and self-depreciating class, others could benefit from their nurturing and support, gaining the opportunity for self-expansion. As long as women were conditioned to be passive and compliant, others could have the opportunity to be active and powerful. Counseling based on models that supported traditional sex role socialization therefore served the interests of men and children rather than the interests of the distressed women.

The recognition that women were not being well served by existing theories and prevailing practices has only become widespread within the last decade. Only during this period has there been a growing awareness that counselors who maintain and reinforce sex role stereotypes often do so to the detriment of their female clients' psychological well-being. Only in this last decade has there been a growing awareness that women's psychological distress is in part attributable to inequitable social structures and institutions and that these inequities require amelioration before women's problems can be totally solved.

With this growing awareness, counselors began increasingly to examine their own notions of what constitutes appropriate behavior for women, what constitutes appropriate opportunities for women's development, and what is the value of women's social contribution. Counselors began to examine how they themselves as well as their female clients internalized socially prescribed notions of appropriateness, notions that restrict women's psychological growth and development. Counselors began to look for ways in which to counteract the negative effects of female sex role socializations while simultaneously recognizing and valuing the positive results of such socialization. Counselors began to look for ways in which they could encourage the total development of their female clients.

The advent of the Women's Movement accelerated this process of counselor reevaluation, as women became more articulate in voicing their dissatisfactions and more assertive in demanding changes. Furthermore, the methods and techniques that were being developed by women in the movement, such as consciousness raising and sharing of common experiences by uninhibited self-disclosure, were methods that were found to be useful adjuncts to counseling, methods that could be modified and incorporated into the counseling process.

Feminist counseling thus evolved from dissatisfaction with traditional counseling theories and practices, from counselors' awareness that they were supporting an inequitable status quo, and from the evolving methods that were found beneficial in supporting and strengthening members of women's groups. Feminist counseling might have begun as a reaction to a traditional sexist counseling mode, but it soon began to develop a theory and a practice that were distinctively its own.

EVOLUTION OF COUNSELING THEORIES

Theories of behavior and behavior change underlie prevailing counseling practices, and these theories reflect the values and philosophies of the theoreticians. Since many behavioral theoreticians have been integrated into the social framework of their times, they have tended to perpetuate the values of the groups with which they identify in society. Frequently this reiteration of values in theory is done without any awareness of the biased perspective that is being incorporated and promulgated.

The bases of traditional counseling theories have been many and varied. Some have posited learning as a primary process with rewards and punishments for behavior being the most salient shaping factor. Other theories have given primacy to the interaction of the emotional with the rational aspects of human thought and behavior. Still others have focused on the irrational and unconscious determinants of behavior. What these theories have commonly shared is an intrapsychic perspective that is based on a male world view. All these theories have looked to internal processes rather than social forces for the primary determinants of behavior. External events may be credited with having some effect on behavior, but the structure of these external events in allowing unequal access to various personal goals is not analyzed. Furthermore, traditional theories are based on an implicit assumption that a male perspective defines the personal and social world while a female perspective lacks validity or is of significantly lesser value. Traditional theories, therefore, and the resultant counseling techniques and skills, have consistently tended to diminish the value and reality of women's perspective on the social order.

Dissatisfaction with these traditional theories of behavior and behavior change has increasingly led some theoreticians to reexamine their assumptions and basic inferences regarding women's psychological growth and development. Some of the traditional counseling theories have in consequence been modified in an attempt to integrate or at least recognize some feminist notions. Most behavioral theories have been examined and modified to remove the most blatant aspects of sexism.

Learning theory has been said to be entirely compatible with a nonsexist approach. Blechman (1980) and Fodor (1974) have both suggested that learning theory is ideally suited to improve the situation of women, as it enables women to learn and develop new skills. This, in turn, allows women to deal more competently with social demands and to resolve sex role conflicts. Blechman has suggested that any hint of sex bias can be eliminated by a thorough functional analysis in problem assessment and by the quantification of observational ratings in behavior monitoring.

While objectivity and reliability of measurement are admirably stressed in counseling modes based on learning theory, this theory pays little attention to the shaping force of the social context in which individual problems and proposed solutions occur. Women's unhappiness may reflect social role expectations that are unrealistic, antagonistic, or inherently demoralizing. Any method of behavioral analysis and goal setting that does not examine these roles or expectations for their sex bias will fail to address the root of the problem. For example, many women seek counseling with the espoused goal of being a better lover, wife, or mother. Behavioral goals can certainly be set to meet these objectives. However, if the behaviors that are increased by a successful behavioral counseling regime are not themselves inherently fulfilling for the woman, or if they are antagonistic to her self-development, then it can be argued that although the behavior changed, the counseling was unsuccessful. Counseling based on learning theory and utilizing behavioral methods is not nonsexist by nature but rather will reflect the participants' sex biases, the counselor's as much as the client's.

Psychoanalytic theory, too, has been modified in recent times in a nonsexist direction (Fried, 1974; Notman, 1982; Sherman, 1980). However, these modifications, which have generally begun to attend to societal influences in shaping behavioral norms, have been subject to widespread criticism. It is argued that any theoretical formulation that has as a basic tenet the biological and psychological inferiority of women cannot by virtue of minor modification become nonsexist (Kaplan & Yasinski, 1980; Rohrbaugh, 1979). Psychoanalytic theory, which still retains a foundation of biological determinism in its most recent modifications, simply does not allow women to be as autonomous, independent, and psychologically whole as men.

Nonsexist modifications have been proposed for most of the traditional and popular theories and methods of behavior change. Counseling based on gestalt theory has reportedly been modified to meet the needs of contemporary women (Brien & Sheldon, 1977). Transactional analysis has been found to be amenable to a feminist perspective (Penn, 1978). Existential counseling has been modified to allow for women's self-validation and freedom from sex role stereotyping (Burlin & Guzetta, 1977).

This process of modifying traditional theories to reflect either nonsexist values or an inkling of feminism, however, presents a number of difficulties. The first difficulty is simply the identification of sexism in a theory. Sex role socialization is such a basic and pervasive force in current thinking that although blatant examples are easily recognized, the more subtle aspects of sexism may easily elude a first view. Repeated examination and analysis are frequently required to detect theoretical notions or evaluations that unjustly discriminate against women. Counselors both in clinical practice and in theoretical considerations need to be continually reexamining their notions of womanhood for traces of sexism rather than relying on a one-time purge of the manifest sexism in the theory.

A second difficulty in modifying traditional theories in the nonsexist direction lies in the intrapsychic nature of most of these theories. Sexism is a social phenomenon that is reflected in social structures and institutions. These structures and institutions exert considerable control over women's behavior. If a theory of behavior does not include an analysis of these social forces, it will not be able to eradicate inherent sexism. Feminism incorporates the personal and political. A purportedly nonsexist approach must take into account the impact of political conditions on the individual.

The third difficulty relates to the basic incompatibility of many basic aspects of traditional theories with the feminist perspective. The intrapsychic focus, as noted above, is one. Another is the finite quality of traditional theories, which is hardly congenial to the transitional approach of feminism in understanding female behavior and behavior change. Traditional theories claim to offer a complete understanding of behavior and to help counselors in becoming experts or authorities on behavior change. Feminist theory, in contrast, is admittedly still evolving, still acquiring knowledge and understanding of the nature of women. Feminist counselors, therefore, are partners with their clients in this search for an understanding of women's experience. The authoritative counseling stance based on traditional theories is simply not compatible with the egalitarian feminist perspective.

Attempts to modify traditional theories in the nonsexist or feminist direction, therefore, have resulted at best in unsatisfactory compromises and at worst in simply token gestures. A theoretical framework is required that incorporates the essential aspects of feminism, that incorporates the personal and political, that addresses behavior change as well as social change, and that allows for continual evolution as women's reality becomes manifest. Only on the basis of such a theory can an effective approach to counseling women be developed.

Feminism has been described as therapeutic in and of itself (Mander & Rush, 1974), as a radical position in a continuum of theoretical bases for counseling (Rawlings & Carter, 1977), and as a necessary underlying attitude in a variety of counseling approaches to women (Sturdivant, 1980). Feminist theory can also be considered an essential framework for understanding women's behavior and situation and a necessary foundation for the development of a comprehensive and effective counseling approach to women.

Feminist theory is admittedly a recent, imperfect, and still evolving phenomenon. Sturdivant (1980) has described the essence of this theory as Woman as Subject. Feminist theory begins with Woman in center stage, in full view as an independent, autonomous being. Womanhood is to be understood for itself, not solely or even primarily in relation to men and children. Womanhood is perceived as activity, not as reactivity. Women's roles are validated as primary, not secondary or auxiliary to the roles of others.

Feminist theory presents a view of womanhood that is contradictory to the prevailing perspective, and it therefore sees social and institutional changes as urgent necessities. Feminist theory analyzes the social forces that maintain, perpetuate, and benefit from women's current devalued social position with a view to identifying these as targets for change. Feminist theory thus subsumes the political perspective within the need for a personal reevaluation of women.

Feminist theory attempts to provide a basic framework for understanding women, a framework that is admittedly still in need of considerable elaboration and modification. It also provides a basis on which to develop a counseling practice that is consistent with the theory. However, feminist theory alone is not sufficient for effective counseling. Theories are by definition high-level abstractions, and such abstractions do not automatically translate themselves into congruent counseling behaviors. Counselors require concrete skills to translate their feminist orientation into effective counseling practices. Sturdivant's (1980) claim that feminist counseling is defined as simply good counseling based on a feminist philosophy is clearly not tenable. A feminist philosophy or orientation is undoubtedly essential, but specific feminist counseling skills form an equally important complement to that philosophy in the configuration of feminist counseling.

FEMINIST COUNSELING SKILLS

As feminist theory has evolved, so has the configuration of skills that define feminist counseling practice. Although any counseling method is composed of a complexity of counselor behaviors and skills, there exists a core of skill in feminist counseling that distinguishes it from other counseling approaches. This core is one that is consistently identified in the literature on feminist counseling and in the discussions of practice by feminist counselors and that is evident in tapes and transcripts of feminist counseling sessions.

A total of five skills define the core of the feminist counseling approach. Each of the skills is clearly rooted in feminist philosophy and is designed to foster feminist counseling goals. Each skill is a describable set of counselor behaviors that can be clearly observed, systematically learned, and purposefully implemented in a client-counselor interaction.

These five core feminist counseling skills are:

1. positive evaluation of women
2. social analysis
3. encouragement of total development
4. self-disclosure
5. behavior feedback

Each of these skills will be thoroughly discussed in the following chapters.

In defining these skills as core feminist counseling skills, it is assumed that the skills appear with a regular frequency in the counseling practice of a proficient feminist counselor. That is not to suggest, however, that each of the skills will be used by each counselor in every interview. Nor is it suggested that having these skills alone in one's repertoire will make one a proficient counselor. These skills are core skills and do not describe the totality of skills or behaviors used by feminist counselors. Furthermore, each skill is best used selectively according to specific client needs, client readiness, type of client problem, and the counselor's own preparedness to engage a particular client.

Specifically, the core skills are meant to supplement and build upon basic or beginning counseling skills. It is assumed that a feminist counselor will already possess the skills to create facilitative counseling conditions. It is assumed that the counselor will be able to communicate to the client feelings of accurate empathy, positive regard, warmth, and congruence. It is further assumed that the counselor will have developed attending skills of questioning, listening, paraphrasing, reflecting, and summarizing to assist in the process of assessing the nature of the problem. Finally, it is assumed that the counselor will have developed skills such as negotiating and contracting to clarify the nature of the counseling encounter with clients.

Feminist counseling skills, therefore, function on a more advanced level and are skills to be used in the action or change phase of counseling rather than in the beginning phase. The place of feminist counseling skills in relation to the total counseling process will be elaborated further in later chapters. Before proceeding to this elaboration, however, counseling terminology must be defined.

COUNSELING, PSYCHOTHERAPY, AND FEMINISM

The feminist intervention process has been referred to as both *feminist counseling* and *feminist psychotherapy*. Since this is potentially confusing, it is worth drawing a distinction between psychotherapy and counseling. Psychotherapy is an intensive process of remediation of psychological dysfunction or adjustment to psychic stressors. Counseling, in contrast, is a more developmental, educational, or preventive process, which is focused on the growing strengths and abilities of the individual in the situation. Feminist counseling transcends the differences between counseling and therapy most distinctively in that it strives to integrate the internal psychic development of women with the opportunities and expectations of their social situation. The goal of feminist counseling is remediation on both the psychological and social levels. Both the internal and external aspects of clients' problems are equally considered in the process. Since this consideration of the external is a distinguishing characteristic, along with the educational-developmental focus, the process is best and most accurately described as *counseling*.

A definition of *counseling* that fits the feminist context is one that has been suggested by Pietrofessa et al. (1978), who call counseling "the professional relationship between a trained help giver and a person in psychological distress seeking help." Proceding from this point, feminist counseling may be defined as a specific type of counseling in the following words:

> A collaborative process between counselor and client in which both identify, analyze, and attempt to remediate the social, cultural, and psychological barriers to women's optimal functioning, setting as the immediate goal the alleviation of the client's personal distress and as the long-term goal the effecting of social change.

Feminist counseling is distinguished from other counseling approaches by its emphasis on the negative psychological aspects of female socialization and by its recognition that counselor and client alike have been subject to this process and must work together to understand and remedy it. Social change along with individual change is seen as necessary to effect a complete and total remedy. It is from these basic premises of social analysis and egalitarianism in the client-counselor relationship that the distinctive skills of feminist counseling are derived.

THEORY, RESEARCH, AND PRACTICE IN FEMINIST COUNSELING

The complete development of any counseling approach requires a clear presentation of its underlying theory and philosophy, an empirical validation of its theoretical postulations, and a clear articulation of skills or counseling behaviors that demonstrate the approach.

Previous presentations of feminist counseling have tended to stress theory and philosophy without sufficiently addressing either research or skills. Although theory is basic to any counseling approach and additional theoretical elaboration is required for feminist counseling, it does not follow that this must precede empirical investigation or development and refinement of counseling practice. On the contrary, practice and research can provide the necessary feedback on which theoretical elaboration can proceed. The optimal development of any counseling approach depends on the integration of theoretical development, practice wisdom, and feedback from empirical evaluation of the effectiveness of the particular elements of the approach. Feminist counseling can benefit from the continual and progressive developments of theory, research, and practice.

The skills that constitute the core of feminist counseling, therefore, will be discussed in terms of their theoretical bases, their practice implications, and the supporting research. The basic theoretical premise upon which the particular skill rests will be presented first. Since the feminist theoretical perspective has been described ably by several feminist counseling authors (Collins, 1982; Rawlings & Carter, 1977; Rohrbaugh, 1979; Sturdivant, 1980), a general discussion will be eschewed here in favor of theoretical positions specific to particular counseling skills.

Following the statement of theoretical positions, discussion of research and other evidence supporting the effectiveness of a skill will be presented in order to provide empirical validation. Not all feminists would agree that empirical validation is called for or is even appropriate for an approach based on a female perspective. Some feminists have argued that the masculine nature of science has developed from an overdependence on empiricism and rationality, with a neglect of the subjective, intuitive, and phenomenological aspects of experience. These feminists have chosen, therefore, to depend on the latter, more feminine, traits and neglect the former. However, this exclusive focus on the subjective and intuitive belies the methodical and rationally developed process of planned change. Neither individual nor social change is likely to occur without rationally planned and focused activity. Empirical evaluation simply serves to make such plans more effective.

Feminist counseling, just like any other counseling approach, needs to be examined in terms of its total effectiveness, in terms of the effectiveness of its component parts, and in terms of its own particular goals. These goals need not be ones derived from a masculine perspective but rather should be ones consistent with a feminist philosophy. Evaluating clinical practice in terms of feminist goals can help counselors to be more effective in making the many judgments and choices presented within a counseling session. Feminist counselors, like other counselors, have an ethical obligation to their clients to strive to improve and develop their counseling practice. This can most effectively be done with the aid of empirical feedback.

Lastly, each skill will be detailed and described in relation to practice applications. Typical applications will be described, and examples of clinical situations will be given. Limitations of skill application in practice will be discussed. Role-playing exercises will be presented to allow rehearsal of each skill in turn. A transcript of an experienced feminist counselor enacting the same role will be presented to allow comparisons of rehearsed role playing with that of a model. Specific counseling responses will be presented, but *not* with the intention that these be learned and recited at appropriate moments. Rather, the hope here is that some familiarity with types of feminist counseling responses will be acquired, so that counselors can then integrate into their own counseling practice those aspects of responses which are compatible with their personal style.

If the development of feminist counseling can be pursued in the three spheres of theory, research, and practice, a more thorough and convincing validation of the approach will ensue. As feminist counseling is increasingly validated, it becomes an exciting and legitimate area of study for counselors of all persuasions. Ultimately, feminist counseling can clearly demonstrate its place as the choice counseling approach for women.

LEARNING FEMINIST COUNSELING SKILLS

Skill acquisition can proceed in several ways. One way to learn a new counseling skill is simply to read about it. For basic, simple skills, this may indeed be sufficient. Another way to learn a counseling skill is to observe a model performing the skill at a high level. From the model observation, one can extract the essential skill elements and then incorporate them into one's own practice.

A third way to learn a skill is by trial and error accompanied by a critique from a warm, supportive supervisor, who provides feedback regarding the merits and inadequacies of the performance. Remedial practice or repeated efforts at skill performance subject to the same critical analysis can then ensue.

All three methods of learning counseling skills have been utilized in counseling training programs. Each of them has been demonstrated to have areas of success. Not surprisingly, however, it is the combination of all three methods—didactic teaching, modeling, and supervision with remedial practice—that has proven most effective.

Microtraining was the term developed by Ivey (1971) to describe this step-by-step learning sequence that followed the delineation of well-defined counseling skills. Ivey recommended a learning sequence that consisted of a baseline, taped, five-minute simulated interview, reading a manual describing the single skill to be learned, observing a model performing the skill, a review of the baseline interview by a supportive supervisor, and a final remedial interview designed to make any changes.

The effectiveness of learning counseling skills by this microtraining method has been repeatedly demonstrated (Danish, D'Augelli & Brock, 1976; Haase & DiMattia, 1970; Moreland, Ivey & Phillips, 1973). In addition, microtraining has been found superior to other approaches such as human relations training (Toukamanian & Rennie, 1975), sensitivity training and programmed learning (Hearn, 1976), and insight-oriented training (Gormally, Hill, Otis & Rainey, 1975).

This combination of didactic instruction, modeling, rehearsal, and remedial practice is therefore recommended as a regimen to learn feminist counseling skills. Each feminist counseling skill to be presented here will be backed by a role-playing exercise and a transcript of a parallel role enacted by an experienced feminist counselor. Role-playing performance can then be compared to the model transcripts, and a critique can be made by the individual, by a supervisor, or by a group of peers. Remedial role playing can then follow.

The value of rehearsal and remedial practice in role playing for skill acquisition cannot be overemphasized. Feminist counseling skills, like any new skills, initially seem awkward and artificial. Role playing can be used to acquire some finesse in skill performance, to modify skill performance in accord with personal counseling style, and to acquire feedback from simulated clients. All this can occur without any damaging or deleterious effects to authentic clients.

Suggested role-playing exercises are presented for each feminist counseling skill at the end of the relevant chapter. Transcripts of feminist counselors enacting the roles follow. Readers and students of feminist counseling skills are strongly advised to use the suggested format to improve their counseling practice.

Chapter 2

GOALS OF FEMINIST COUNSELING

FEMINIST COUNSELING GOALS DEFINED

Feminist counseling is an approach that was developed specifically for women, that incorporates a particular philosophy about women, and that has a political as well as an individual perspective on women's problems. It follows, therefore, that the goals of feminist counseling are distinct in pertaining to the unique condition of women both individually and collectively.

Women seek counseling for a variety of reasons, not all of which are specifically gender related. Frequently, women seek counseling because they are experiencing distressful negative feelings about themselves or about their relationships with others. These distressful feelings can be generated by frustrated or conflictual expectations—expectations of oneself, expectations of others, others' expectations of oneself. Expectations of this nature almost invariably are gender related.

Women's expectations of themselves tend to be congruent with social role definitions, such as that of wife, mother, lover, daughter, and so on. Likewise, others' expectations of a particular woman tend to be congruent with their expectations of women at large. Expectations of women can serve as social barriers restricting women's functioning. These barriers frequently are attributed to women's intrinsic limitations but in fact often serve more pragmatic purposes. For example, women are exhorted to remain home with young children to fulfill their "maternal instinct" and to fulfill expectations of "good mothering." Simultaneously, however, by remaining at home, women are excluded from job competition with men and placed in a dependent position in society.

Feminist counseling goals eschew these social definitions and gender-related limitations and instead focus on promoting maxi-

20

mal personal development and social influence of women. Feminist counseling goals, therefore, include the promotion of independence, autonomy, and personal effectiveness. These goals are common to other counseling approaches as well, but in feminist counseling they are pursued simultaneously with the goal of providing a feminist social perspective. This additional goal aids clients not only in dealing with their particular situations but also in recognizing areas requiring social change.

The common counseling goals of independence, autonomy, and personal effectiveness have a somewhat different meaning, derived from the feminist perspective, in feminist counseling. Their specific connotations are:

1. Independence—having validity in and of oneself as a woman, a sense of oneself as complete without endorsement from others, a positive image of one's own worth including one's female assets; having the ability to see oneself in center stage with one's own needs and goals as foremost and central to self-fulfillment.

2. Autonomy—having and using the ability to direct one's own life, to make one's own decisions, to take action on one's own behalf and not only to react to others; taking responsibility for one's behavior and emotions instead of blaming others; exerting open and direct influence instead of pursuing covert and manipulative change efforts; joining with others to exert social power when social changes are necessary to fulfill personal needs and goals.

3. Personal effectiveness—being androgynous in the sense of combining male and female qualities within oneself; repossessing and developing those aspects of oneself previously rejected or ignored because of their masculine connotations; acquiring required skills and behaviors to make oneself more effective personally and socially.

Feminist counseling goals, therefore, are similar to general counseling goals but have undergone a shift in emphasis, a redirection from the typical goal of "adjustment to the situation" to a redefinition of the situation and the woman's place in it. Feminist counseling goals do not fit a woman to her situation but rather help her understand the situation. They also aim to provide her with skills, competencies, and confidence to change the situation into one of equitability for herself and for women generally.

While feminist counseling goals may be at odds in some ways with the traditional social order, they are not necessarily revolutionary in the sense of seeking to destroy that social order. Rather, feminist counseling goals may be seen to be evolutionary in that they seek to redefine the social order. This difference is sometimes not well understood, and misconceptions about feminist counseling abound. Before discussing the specifics of feminist counseling, these misconceptions need to be laid to rest.

COMMON MISCONCEPTIONS OF FEMINIST COUNSELING GOALS

The term *feminist* in common usage has many different meanings and includes pervasive negative connotations in conjunction with more positive ones. Many of the negative stereotypes regarding feminism relate to its supposed anti-male bias. This perception of feminism as hostile toward men derives in part from its decidedly pro-female stance. Feminism requires a redistribution of power and responsibility between the sexes. This clearly will have an impact on men, but the impact in not necessarily negative. Reduction in power and privilege may well be offset by increased freedom and an increased sense of partnership with women. The ultimate goal is the achievement of fairness and equality for all. The process of reaching this goal, however, may involve conflict and dispute as entrenched positions are redefined.

Feminist counseling is based on the belief that inequality between the sexes currently exists, has existed in the past, and will continue to exist in the future unless positive action is taken to remedy it. Feminist counseling requires more than an impartial stance, more than a gender-fair or nonsexist stance, which ignores women's history. Treating both sexes equally in the present denies the inequality that is part of women's social and individual history. Ultimately, a nonsexist world is desirable, but it must be preceded by a reevaluation and recognition of the contribution and assets of women, by a redistribution of power and responsibility, and by an increased opportunity for female development. Feminist counseling is continually mindful of the obvious, blatant devaluation and restriction of women as well as the subtle, obscure constricting influences and strives to combat these as part of the process of personal and social change.

Feminism in counseling does not strive to exclude men or to isolate women from men. Reevaluation and redefinition of women's relationships with men are important elements in feminist counseling, and while this clearly involves men, it begins with women. Women must first clarify what they want and need from their relationships with men, as opposed to what they have been socialized to expect. Only with some clarity about themselves can women renegotiate with others about relationships. Individual counseling with women may need to precede relationship counseling, even when the distress relates particularly to the relationship. The goal of such counseling would be to help women effectively meet their own needs in the relationship without necessarily diminishing or destroying the relationship. .

This redefinition of female-male relationships may initially be threatening to some men who perceive the continuation of the relationship as dependent on their domination. It may be difficult for some men, themselves molded by social values, to see that a more egalitarian relationship with a more equitable power allocation can be to their benefit. They may find it difficult to accept that partnerships are more satisfying than subservient relationships. Feminist counseling, while being pro-female, ultimately has benefits for men as well.

Another misconception about feminist counseling is that it strives to replace male domination of women by female domination of men. This misconception arises from feminism's acknowledged goal of regaining female power. Feminist counseling aims to have women recognize their strengths, to maximize the use of latent traits and competencies, and to develop skills and abilities that will increase flexibility and independence. Independence does not, however, mean isolation or domination. Feminist counseling does not aim to have women supplant men or to have women become interchangeable with men. The goal, rather, is to have cooperative and flexible relationships wherein roles can be either equivalent or complementary, with none of the stresses of hierarchical relationships.

Another misconception about feminist counseling is that it strives to have all women abrogate their homemaking and child-rearing functions in favor of the competitive functions of the marketplace. This misconceptions arises from a hasty understanding of the feminist goal of increased choice for women. In the past, women have had little choice about their roles, and given the diversity in individual women's abilities and interests, it is not surprising that psychological distress has ensued. Not all women are suited for homemaking, just as not all women are suited for executive functioning. Feminist counseling strives to evaluate positively the contribution of women in whatever arena they choose and to provide women with maximum choices. Feminist counseling aims to bring to an end the allocation of roles and functions on the basis of gender and instead to allow interests, abilities, and personal choice to determine women's course in life.

Feminist counseling goals, therefore, are not anti-men, anti-motherhood, or anti-homemaking. Feminist counseling goals do, however, emphasize strength and competency and discourage dependency, subservience, and submission.

Feminist counseling is counseling of women by women for women. It is decidedly pro-female in that it seeks the betterment of women individually and collectively and recognizes that this requires both individual and social change.

WHY COUNSELING OF WOMEN ONLY?

Theoretical Background

Traditional solutions to alleviating psychological distress have been based on the medical model, which postulated a problem or "disease" with one specific cause or origin. Once the cause was diagnosed, a corresponding remedy or cure could be applied. Psychological problems frequently were thought to arise from a developmental deficit or dysfunction. Freud's theory of psycho-sexual development, for example, posited a model of libidinal attachments that, when they conflicted with or were derailed by societal sexual inhibitions, resulted in hysterical or psychosomatic complaints. Other psychoanalytic theories of the time posited other basic deficits: Adler perceived a basic sense of inferiority as a primary underlying cause, and Jung perceived the basic deficit as relating to primitive archetypes. More current theories, such as Skinnerian behavior modification, eschew the intrapsychic origins of problems but replace them with a different single deficit, such as learning. All these theories prescribe specific, but different, solutions, with each solution aimed at remedying the specific primary deficit espoused by the theory.

In recent times, however, psychotherapy research has cast doubt on the efficacy of a unicausal model of psychological distress. It has become clear that no treatment approach based on a single-deficit hypothesis has come close to being totally effective with all types of clients and all types of problems. Variable rates of psychotherapy effectiveness have been demonstrated across types of therapy, clients, problems, and therapists (Bergin & Lambert, 1978). The conclusion reached by researchers such as Gottman and Markman (1978) was that a multimodal counseling model was required. Empirical evaluation could then determine the most effective counseling mode for a specific client with a specific problem by a specific type of counselor. Increasingly, the literature on counseling and psychotherapy practice is also beginning to reflect this perspective.

In general, any given client group is best served by a counseling approach that addresses its specific problems, deficits, and developmental history. Women, as a group, have been badly served in the past by existing counseling approaches, which were totally lacking in a female perspective. Existing counseling theories were based on a male world view. Most blatantly so were the psychoanalytic theories, which held women's psychosexual development to be invariably and inevitably deficient due to their lack of a penis. Personal fulfillment for women was possible only partially and by proxy in the guise of having a male child. Support of such a perspective was offered by statements of little girls who wished for such an appendage. An explanation of this kind has as much logical value as that of a developmental theory posited on the oft-expressed childhood desire to fly—a theory explaining distress on the basis of frustrated desires to be feathered and airborne!

Other theories marketing the desirability of adjusting to social norms, either explicitly or implicitly, have molded women into forms deemed desirable by men. When societal needs, or the needs of the prevailing male majority, conflicted with women's individual needs, the latter were inevitably sacrificed. Women who persisted in pursuing their own needs and women who questioned the status quo were marked with psychological labels that denoted individual pathology, social deviance, or at least personal malfunctioning.

Consequently, women, who were seeking counseling in ever-increasing numbers due to stress emanating in part from social conditions, were counseled to adjust to and accept those same conditions. It is no wonder that depression and anxiety became women's habitual state.

Theories relating to female development and female social functioning have largely been generated by men and have perceived female functioning in negative and pejorative terms. Female reproductive functions, which have no masculine parallel in terms of complexity, have been treated as taboos or illnesses. Pregnancy, menstruation, and lactation have been sources of female shame and sorrow rather than pride and joy. Femininity has been defined instead as those giving, nurturing, pleasing behaviors that serve primarily to satisfy men.

Psychological theories relating to mothering have stressed the psychopathology that can ensue from women's interaction with their children, especially their sons. Either mothers are overprotective and do not allow their children to separate and develop, or they are cold, distant, and neglectful and do not meet their children's emotional needs. The father, in these psychological analyses, is always conspicuously absent, frequently because the mother is an "overfunctioner" who prevented his involvement. Mothers, according to these theories, do nothing but harm and are totally responsible for all resulting familial distress.

Woman as wife fares no better in the psychotherapeutic literature. The alcoholic husband is inevitably linked to a wife who, if not causing the situation, is gleefully and needfully perpetuating it. Depression and suicide in males are not infrequently linked to the cold, uncaring wife. Even in old age, problems of male adjustment to retirement are theoretically exacerbated (if not caused) by the wife's unwillingness to relinquish her control of the domestic domain.

There has been a total lack of theories that relate to a woman's view of the world, stress the positive aspects of female functioning, value women's contribution to the social fabric, and regard their expressive functions as equal to or greater than predominantly male instrumental functions. It is only in the last decade that women have started to reevaluate their roles and functions and have begun to develop a positive female image. Women are just beginning to recognize the need for a redefinition of the world from the female perspective and the need for theories that relate female functions to health and power, not illness and despair.

Concurrently with this recognition of the need for redefined theories has come the recognition of corresponding counseling practices. Counseling practices based on women's needs and with demonstrable positive outcomes for women are sorely required. Traditional counseling practices simply do not suffice.

Traditional Counseling Practice

Traditional therapeutic and counseling practices have had a sorry record in relation to producing positive changes in and for women. Women have been exploited not only psychologically in traditional counseling but often sexually as well. All of this was done in the name of helping the client. Women were counseled repeatedly and consistently to adjust to prevailing social situations, even when these were clearly unjust and pathogenic. The increase in the number of women being treated for recurring episodes of depression bespeaks a counseling system that fails to meet client needs.

The past two decades have seen the emergence of some counseling approaches that have striven to alleviate the most blatant negative biases toward women. Nonsexist theories have emerged, gender-fair approaches have been espoused, and counselors have consciously striven to treat their female clients on par with their male clients. However, in spite of counselor's best intentions, there is little evidence that a truly effective counseling approach can be developed by simply eliminating the most blatant and glaring aspects of a sex bias. Sexism is such an inherent aspect of the social fabric, such an integral part of our conceptualization of men and women, that it is unlikely that a superficial sweep of sexist thinking can truly eliminate a counselor's sexist biases. Furthermore, even if it were possible to eliminate these from the counseling encounter, sexual discrimination and oppression remain in society, and women's opportunities and possibilities remain restricted when compared to those of men. A nonsexist counseling approach does not address these inequities.

What is required is a counseling approach based on a conscious and continual examination and elimination of sexist biases, a conscious and continual reexamination of the value of female roles and functions, and a consideration of individual sexism, social sexism, and the interaction between the two. Feminist counseling is a counseling approach of women that incorporates the personal and political aspects of female functioning, with the aim of not only eliminating sexist biases but also fostering a female perspective of the world that acknowledges the central place of women in such a world. Feminist counseling is counseling of women in the most total and positive sense of the word.

WHY COUNSELING BY WOMEN ONLY?

Theoretical Background

Phyllis Chesler (1970) was one of the first outspoken advocates of female counselors for female clients. Her argument was that since male counselors had repeatedly exploited their female clients both psychologically and sexually, the opportunity for this could immediately be rescinded by having only female counselors for female clients. Many feminist counselors have supported this position. These counselors have recognized that the amelioration of overt and covert sexism is more likely to be achieved if a counselor has experienced it herself. Sexism in so pervasive, so subtle, and so well integrated into women's behavior that it is only by constant reexamination of one's own behavior patterns coupled with challenges from other women that the vestiges of such influences can be uncovered.

That is not to say, however, that female counselors are superior to male counselors in all situations at all times. Male counselors can and do practice feminist counseling, while many female counselors perpetuate sexism in their counseling practice. Furthermore, the present reality is that many counseling services are still provided by men. They as well as their female colleagues need to be retrained in the feminist perspective.

Types of problems presented by clients vary in their sensitivity to the need for gender-matched counselors. Problems relating to sex role definition, role transition, or reevaluation of roles and status are ones in which female counselors are more critical for female clients. However, problems related to more practical issues, such as housing, finances, medical services, and employment, may be less sensitive to counselor gender. Even in dealing with these practical issues, however, awareness of sex role differences is important.

In a specific counseling situation, the counselor's awareness of sexism and his or her individual attitudes toward women may be more important than gender. However, female counselors, as a group, do have the potential to be more sensitive to these issues by virtue of their life experiences and the experience of female socialization. Research evidence supports this contention in indicating that women indeed tend to be less sexist than men.

Attitudinal Research

While it is true that each counselor must be examined on her or his own merits, attitudinal research has consistently documented that male counselors have more sexist attitudes than female counselors. Broverman et al.'s (1970) study of mental health practitioners found that all counselors had sexist notions of healthy adult functioning and that this did not vary by counselor gender. This finding, however, has not been consistently replicated. In testing it, Harris and Lucas (1976), for example, found no overall differences in social work students' definition of healthy adults but did find that female students rated adult women as healthier than

did male students. Brown and Hellinger (1975) surveyed 274 Cana-
dian counselors and found female counselors share contemporary
attitudes toward women while male counselors have more traditional and restrictive attitudes. Abramowitz et al. (1976) presented
fictitious case material to 112 practicing counselors and found that
female counselors were overall more empathic than male counselors,
particularly with female clients. Sherman, Koufacos, and Kenworthy
(1978) presented questionnaires to 184 counselors and found female counselors to be better informed, more liberal, and less
stereotyped than male counselors in their views about women.
Male counselors, for example, strongly endorsed the statement
that one of the most important goals of counseling was to have
clients adjust to their circumstances. Finally, Billingsley (1977)
found that in selecting treatment goals for clients, female counselors
selected more masculine goals for their female clients, while male
counselors selected more traditional female goals.

The trend is clear that in the aggregate, male counselors hold
more conservative or more sexist attitudes toward women than do
female counselors. However, even among female counselors there
is a considerable range in attitudes. Bosma (1975) found in a study
of fifteen female counselors that half identified themselves as
feminists and that these feminist counselors defined a client's
strengths in terms of her ability to define and assert herself. The
nonfeminist counselors, on the other hand, defined client strength
in terms of motivation for counseling. Furthermore, the feminist
counselors also perceived their female clients as less ill and more
competent than the nonfeminist female counselors did. The gender of the counselor, therefore, is no guarantee of liberal attitudes
toward women.

Attitudes toward women are clearly in transition, but here
again it has been demonstrated that female counselors are changing their attitudes more rapidly and more broadly than male
counselors. Engelhard, Jones, and Stiggins (1976) measured attitudes toward women in a random sample of guidance counselors
in 1968, 1971, and 1975 and found that all counselors had become more liberal over this period. All had come to be more
accepting of working mothers and had developed a broader sex
role definition for women. However, female counselors had be-

come significantly more liberal in their attitudes than their male counterparts. Additionally, on measuring the social impact or evaluation of female social contributions, little change over time was detected, but female counselors consistently scored significantly higher than male counselors.

A number of reviewers of attitudinal research (Abramowitz & Dokecki, 1977; Stricker, 1977) have argued that although female and male counselors may demonstrate differential sex role attitudes on paper and pencil measures, there is no evidence that these attitudes are translated into differential treatment effects. However, it seems quite illogical to negate the effects of attitudes in the context of counseling when attitudes are accepted as important and significant predictors of behavior in other areas of psychology. Furthermore, there is enough evidence in studies of counseling outcome to suggest that for at least some types of female clients, the gender of the counselor can be a very important variable.

Clinical Research

Traditional female socialization stresses interpersonal and affiliative goals over achievement goals, and women are taught to be responsive to others even at the expense of their own needs. Since they are aware of this kind of pervasive influence, female counselors may be expected to be more reponsive and sensitive to clients' feelings and more emotionally in tune with their clients (Carter, 1971; Krause, 1975). Clinical research indicates that while female counselors are not necessarily more effective and more empathic with all clients, they do have a decided advantage with specific client groups.

In a post hoc analysis of the records of 147 women who had attended a mental health clinic between 1965 and 1967, Orlinsky and Howard (1980) found that female counselors tended to be significantly more effective with young, single female clients than were male counselors. With other client groups, counselor gender was not a relevant factor in outcome determination. For the young, female client, the element of role modeling by a more mature female may be a particularly important factor.

Clinical assessments by counselors can also vary by counselor gender. Haan and Livson (1973) reanalyzed data from a longitudinal personality study and found that female psychologists saw their female clients as being more intellectually competent and self-accepting than did male psychologists who were making parallel assessments of the same clients.

The counseling process also tends to be more satisfying to clients and more productive when client and counselor are matched by gender. Hill (1975) found that gender-matched client-counselor pairs had more discussion of feelings overall than had nonmatched pairs. Persons, Persons, and Newmark (1974) found that among college students, female clients with a female counselor felt that their counselor was more perceptive and insightful, encouraged more risk taking, was more warm and friendly, was more helpful with sexual identity concerns, gave more honest feedback, was more self-disclosing, and was more supportive than did those with a male counselor. Male clients similarly found male counselors more helpful along many of the same dimensions. Again it seems that role modeling and an appreciation of sex role socialization may be important factors in determining client satisfaction.

Although some reviewers have concluded that this evidence is scanty (Tanney & Birk, 1978), a clear trend does emerge indicating that young, female clients are more satisfied with and benefit more from female counselors. The evidence of role modeling and sex role socialization strongly suggests that female clients in any role transition may be best served by female counselors. Female counselors can utilize their own experience in role transition to provide clients at once with empathy and understanding as well as a role model.

In summary, female clients tend to be more satisfied with and to benefit more from counseling with a female counselor. That does not mean, however, that an individual male counselor may not be effective. Nor does it mean that all female counselors are effective simply by virtue of their gender. It is probably truer that particular types of female clients, such as young women still defining their feminine role and women in various role transitions, are best served by female counselors with an awareness of sex role issues. For other female clients, the gender of the counselor may not be as critical. However, given the pervasive nature of our sex role socialization, even that statement must await more extensive empirical validation.

Clinical Practice

Clients in many instances have little choice in the type of counseling they will receive or the gender of the counselor providing it. This is particularly true in public agencies, where case assignment may be done by random choice, by geographic expediency, or by types of problems and may bear no relation to the clients' needs or interests.

Knowledgeable counselors, therefore, have the responsibility of educating their agencies, their colleagues, and their clients about the benefits of gender-matched counseling. On the agency level, case assignment procedures can be revised to maximize the likelihood of gender matching, particularly with young adult clients. Obviously, limited resources may not always allow such matching, but the intent can be documented in policy statements.

Colleagues can also be influenced to maximize their awareness of feminist issues and the desirability of gender matching with clients. Peer reviews of case management, case presentation of female clients encumbered by sex role socialization, informal discussions of women's issues, and guest presentations by feminist counselors are some of the many ways in which colleagues can be sensitized to sex role dilemmas of typical clients. Sexist practice in many instances simply reflects lack of knowledge about alternate counseling approaches or lack of attention to sexism in counseling. Many counselors have been indoctrinated with the basic client-centered reflective approach and may simply be unaware of more active, reeducative counseling alternatives. Other counselors may simply have neglected to consider the sexist bias inherent in client problems and situations. Sharing of information and counseling experiences by feminist counselors can help to broaden the perspectives of colleagues and co-workers.

Clients also need to be advised of relevant information regarding counselor choice. A number of recent publications such as *A Woman's Guide to Therapy* by Friedman et al. (1979) and *The New*

Woman's Survival Sourcebook (1975) advise clients about those characteristics and approaches of counselors which might be relevant. While not all such guides emphasize counselor gender, a client needs to consider the effect of matched or nonmatched gender on her comfort and satisfaction in receiving counseling. Female clients at times may ask for male counselors, as they perceive men to be more expert, more trustworthy, and more attractive (Feldstein, 1982). Although such choices must be respected, it should be ensured that these choices are made following consideration of available information about possible outcomes. Counselors with knowledge about the benefits of gender matching have the responsibility of sharing it with their clients as well as their colleagues and their agencies.

WHY A COUNSELING APPROACH FOR WOMEN?

Background Theory

One of the most common objections to feminist counseling is that it perpetuates sexism. Inasmuch as both males and females are subject to restricting sex role socialization, it is claimed that a more equitable counseling approach is a nonsexist or gender fair approach. Furthermore, it is argued that a counseling approach designed to benefit primarily women simply augments and perpetuates sexist social divisions and inequities.

There is no doubt that sex role socialization does indeed restrict men's choices as well as women's, but male socialization continues to work to men's advantage by fostering attitudes, behaviors, and skills that are primarily beneficial for men. Women, on the other hand, are socialized to acquire behaviors and attitudes that primarily benefit others. Their passivity and submission benefit the people in charge, and the people in charge are usually men. Nurturance obviously benefits the recipient more than the provider, and the cost of providing nurturance may be considerable self-denial.

Female socialization has other negative consequences as well, which have no parallel in male socialization. Direct exercise of power is discouraged, and this gives rise to indirect female strategies. These indirect strategies frequently lead to extreme dependence upon the unpredictable and ultimately uncontrollable behavior of others. Women who can only have their needs met through the behavior of husbands or children must invest a great deal of energy into attempting to influence these others. Since such efforts have to be disguised, they are frequently ignored, displaced, or resented. Even when successful, indirect influence garners women little credit. Neither men nor children like to be reminded that their achievements were fostered by the support, encouragement, and ancillary services provided by women.

Not only does this indirect use of power provide little satisfaction for women, but also it prohibits the development of direct modes of communication and influence. Women, therefore, are frequently restricted to this less effective mode of influence, whereas men have both greater choices about uses of power and more opportunities to exercise power.

Women are penalized in sex role socialization in many ways that men are not. Women, therefore, need a counseling approach that does not simply regard women as equal to men but rather encourages women to analyze their situation in terms of internalized sex role limitations and inhibitions. Women need to be encouraged to shift their socialized deference to others into an increased attention to the self. Women need to be encouraged to develop skills that will increase their flexibility to cope with a wide range of situations. Lastly, women require a counseling approach that will affirm their value and contribution as women instead of relegating them to second-class status. It is by incorporating these elements that feminist counseling becomes counseling of women.

Clinical Practice

Counseling practice with women requires an active participation by both counselor and client. Feminist counseling is a process whereby client and counselor together identify the sex-related constraints on the client and try to eliminate them. Feminist counseling, therefore, involves the counselor to a significantly greater extent than more traditional approaches in which the counselor may be more remote.

Feminist counselors are critically aware that their personal biases, opinions, and values will influence the client-counselor interaction regardless of how much they try to negate these factors. Feminist counselors reject the notion of "value-free" counseling, or the notion that counseling is a value-free application of techniques and skills. Instead, there is agreement with the observations of Bart (1971), Bernard (1969), and Hurvitz (1973), all of whom describe traditional counseling as serving the function of social control, of adjustment to frequently intolerable social situations. Such counseling is clearly far from value-free.

Feminist counselors are therefore clear about communicating counseling goals and their underlying values to their clients. Furthermore, feminist counselors understand that information about the feminist perspective and its bearings upon a client's situation needs to be communicated to clients to enlarge their alternatives and options. The feminist counselor is therefore consciously and deliberatively active in presenting a feminist perspective to her clients. That is not to say that the feminist counselor bombards the client with feminist rhetoric. Rather, the counselor sensitively introduces points of view that encourage the client to see her problem as having sex role components common to all women and shows that these will not be totally remedied until large-scale social changes are effected.

The feminist counselor's role is therefore an educative as well as a supportive one. The counselor utilizes information about the status of women in society, sharing this with her client as it is appropriate and relevant to the client's situation. Some of this information may be factual, such as the increasing wage disparity between men and women; other presentations may be more political or philosophical, such as the sexual objectification and exploitation of women by men. The goal of this information sharing is not to induce rage against men or the prevailing social system (although these reactions may temporarily ensue) but rather to demonstrate that women as a group are subject to particular stresses and that the client's problems reflect an aspect of this larger problem. The need for client change is not denied but simply put into a larger social context.

Since feminist counselors are more active, more educative, and more self-revealing than traditional counselors, there is increased likelihood that clients will begin to see their counselors as role models. That is not to suggest that feminist counselors set themselves up as models for emulation but rather to say that they are willing to share common experiences and common ordeals and admit to grappling with common issues to indicate that there are a variety of ways, admittedly imperfect at present, of dealing with such situations. Particularly for women in role transition, it can be helpful to know that another woman has passed through that change, has survived, and perhaps has profited from it.

Feminist counseling is, therefore, counseling in which counselors assume the role of information provider, social analysis presenter, self-discloser, and profferer of encouragement. Feminist counselors cannot afford to sit back and simply empathize and reflect back client statements, although much of this occurs in the early stages of all counseling. Just as feminist counselors encourage clients to take greater hold of their lives, to be more assertive, more critical of sex role stereotypes, so must feminist counselors themselves be more active, open, and socially analytical within the counseling process. Admittedly, feminist counselors vary considerably in individual counseling styles, but an emphasis on an egalitarian and involving style is common. Not only is feminist philosophy promoted by such counseling, but generally a keener interest and enjoyment of the process can also be anticipated.

ETHICAL ISSUES IN FEMINIST COUNSELING

Freedom of Choice

Feminist counselors who maintain a staunch position of feminist advocacy with all clients do so on the basis of an assumption of informed and free client choice. The assumption is made that if the client is not comfortable with a feminist analysis, if the client does not wish to pursue feminist goals, or if the client finds the counselor too radical, she will simply not engage with the counselor but will seek help elsewhere. This assumption, however, is subject to numerous restraints. Clients experiencing considerable psycho-logical distress and pain may not have the energy or motivation to search out alternate counselors. Since many clients are not aware of the differences between various counseling orientations, they assume that all counselors offer similar services. Clients may require immediate intervention, and the time may not be appro-priate for discussing differences in counseling theories and practices. These reasons apart, either geographic or economic necessities may dictate a client's choice of counselor.

Feminist counselors, particularly those working in public agen-cies, are frequently faced with the obligation of providing a serv-ice that is generic in nature. While feminism is not an attribute that can be rescinded at will, it is true that neither all clients nor all situations require a full-fledged feminist analysis. Clients firmly entrenched in sex role stereotypes can be helped by feminist counselors without being threatened or put on the defensive. Feminist counselors have an obligation to expand the perspectives of their clients, but this expansion can simply be through the presentation of a wider range of alternatives or through a discus-sion of alternate perspectives without undue emphasis or stress on feminist options. The rights of clients to make personal choices, even when these may seem unwise, must always be respected.

Influence and Direction in Counseling

Feminist counselors, then, attempt to direct clients to a specific type of social and personal cognition. To counselors trained in a more traditional, nondirective approach, this may appear to di-minish the self-determination of clients.

However, in reality, counselor influence pervades even the most nondirective approaches. All counselors are perceived as authorities, experts in human relations, and skilled practitioners in problem solving by their clients. As such, both verbal and nonverbal counselor responses have considerable significance. Counselors are continually selective in their responses — they de-cide *when* to respond, *how* to respond, and *with what* to respond. Clients are attuned to these responses and place considerable weight on even the slightest of responses. Counselors simply cannot avoid influencing or directing their clients even when they maintain that their influence is negligible.

Counselor influence has been empirically demonstrated in a number of clinical studies. In investigating changing client values throughout counseling, several studies have found that clients who increasingly adopt their counselor's values are more likely to be considered "successful" or improved (Landfield & Nawas, 1964; Welkowitz, Cohen & Ortmeyer, 1966). Feminist counselors, unlike some others, acknowledge the reality of this influence and make it known to their clients.

Feminist counseling theory does not flinch from a discussion of influence, power, and choice in counseling. It recognizes the power of the counselor, the particular direction of that influence, and the poverty of choices aviavable to many clients. Feminist counseling promotes open discussion of these issues with clients as opposed to repression or diversion of them from the counseling encounter. It can indeed be argued that in being clear about influence, power, and choice, feminist counseling is promoting a more ethical stance in relation to clients than are other counseling approaches. Certainly there is no attempt to subvert client rights or manipulate them indirectly, which occurs when issues of control are not addressed. Feminist counseling has the goal of assisting women to regain their power and starts on that road by being open with clients about the nature of the counseling encounter. This is a position that other counseling approaches might with profit emulate.

Chapter 3

FEMINIST COUNSELING SKILLS IN CONTEXT

PHASES OF COUNSELING

Counseling is a progressively phased process. It begins with an introductory or relationship-building phase. This is followed by an intensive change-oriented or action phase. The process concludes with a termination, leave-taking, or consolidating phase. All counseling modes include these phases, but the duration, content, and relative importance of each phase varies among counseling modalities.

Although counseling phases are described as distinctive, sequential, and progressive, in the clinical situation there is considerable ebb and flow in their progression. Exploration and facilitation, which are the primary tasks of the beginning phase, continue into the latter phases of counseling. Similarly, change-oriented interactions typical of the work phase of counseling frequently occur as well in the beginning and even termination phases. The tasks associated with leave taking and consolidation typical of the termination phase likewise may enter earlier counseling phases. In spite of these overlaps, however, progress in counseling does depend on the tasks of each phase being addressed in turn as the counseling relationship develops.

Feminist counseling is most clearly distinguished from other counseling approaches by the unique characteristics of its change-oriented phase. The beginning phase of feminist counseling is similar to other counseling approaches, but, even there, certain distinctive features can be seen.

THE BEGINNING PHASE IN FEMINIST COUNSELING

The primary tasks of the beginning phase of counseling are the development of a thorough assessment of the presenting problem and a communication of interest, concern, and understanding to the client in relation to her problems. Skills of attending to the client and of communicating facilitative conditions are equally essential to the establishment of this beginning, since they provide the foundation upon which effective counseling can be built.

Attending skills, which have been thoroughly described by Allen Ivey and his associates (Ivey & Authier, 1978; Ivey & Gluckstern, 1976; Ivey & Simek-Downing, 1980), include skills such as paraphrasing, reflection of feeling, minimal encouragement, open questioning, and summarization. These counseling skills promote client problem exploration, which can be used to formulate appropriate counseling change goals. Effective counseling is dependent on the depth and intensity of client self-exploration (Truax & Carkhuff, 1967).

Concepts of facilitative conditions of counseling that promote the development of a positive client-counselor relationship originated with Carl Rogers's (1957) work. They have been elaborated primarily by Truax and Carkhuff (1967). These skills, which are now considered essential to effective counseling, include communication of accurate empathy, positive regard, warmth, genuineness, and concreteness. A counselor who conveys these conditions to her client assures the client of her concern, her willingness and ability to help, and her caring and acceptance of the client as an individual. The establishment of such a relationship is necessary for effective counseling.

Feminist counselors, like all other counselors, need to develop proficiency in attending skills and the skills of promoting facilitative conditions. Ineptness at this beginning phase may result in client dropouts or minimal client engagement in the counseling relationship. Either of these outcomes would preclude clients' acquiring the potential benefits of the action or work phase of feminist counseling.

The attending and facilitative skills are common to most counseling approaches, but in feminist counseling they take on the distinctive flavor of feminist philosophy. Attending by feminist counselors, for example, means not only attending to what the client is saying and doing but also attending closely to the experience of womanhood that is being revealed. Feminist counselors who are trying to develop an understanding of women's world view need to listen closely to each individual woman describe her experience of womanhood. These descriptions coupled with the counselor's own experience can then be integrated into a more encompassing understanding of the female condition.

Attending and facilitating skills in feminist counseling may relate equally to the individual experience of the client and to the more general condition of women. Some examples of how feminist counselors interweave the notion of common womanhood into the reflection of feeling are as follows:

Client: I feel frustrated because there is so little I can do. My husband makes all the important decisions.

Counselor: I can see that you are feeling powerless as a woman who is in the position of having to acquiesce to a husband with all the legitimate power. It is a pretty frustrating experience!

Client: He makes me so mad! He never seems to care about my feelings.

Counselor: I hear you saying that it makes you angry that he, as a man, is not as sensitive to your feelings as you, as a woman, are to his.

Likewise the communication of positive regard can be linked to the commonality of womanhood, as illustrated in the following example:

Client: I feel like a total failure. I don't seem to do anything right anymore.

Counselor: I can understand that you would feel that way since you get so little in the way of positive feedback from others. That tends to be the common lot of women. I, however, see that you are a very capable, able woman who has done a great deal in her life.

Client: I've been so dumb, letting Joe run my life all the time.

Counselor: That's not unusual for women, letting a man take charge. You've just taken a big step in recognizing it and wanting to do something to change it.

Similarly, in using other attending and facilitating skills, feminist counselors introduce their feminist perspective, thereby allowing clients to feel the commonality of womanhood, the validity of their experiences, and the partnership of client and counselor in trying to understand and remedy the negative consequences of these experiences.

Feminist counseling introduces one additional task into the beginning phase of counseling. This task is to let the client know that a feminist analysis will be pursued throughout the counseling encounter. Feminist counselors recognize the potent impact of counselor values and attitudes on the counseling encounter and therefore clearly explicate their feminist position rather than allowing it to influence the counseling process covertly. The manner in which this is communicated, however, can vary to suit both the needs of the individual client as well as the style of the particular counselor.

Most women seeking counseling today are aware in one way or another of the changing social expectations of women. Many women, in fact, recognize and voice the relationship of these changing expectations to their own problems. Most female clients will not be surprised when a counselor makes links between their problems and the common condition of women. Similarly, couples or families seeking counseling tend not to find this analysis unexpected. Families and spouses will not infrequently blame their distress on the woman's changing notions of the female role.

Feminist counselors most effectively present their feminist perspective in terms of expanded options and opportunities for women rather than a new set of prescriptions related to a feminist stereotype. Feminist counseling does not prescribe the abdication of the traditional stereotype for the espousal of a feminist one. Rather, the goal is always to enlarge and increase options for women, and this concept of *enlargement* is the most significant to communicate to clients. The client's freedom of choice is always increased, never restricted, by a feminist analysis.

A counselor may explicate a feminist analysis as follows:

Client: I'm confused about my future. I want to get married now and start a family, but I worry about interrupting my education.

Counselor: I'm not surprised that you are confused and worried. Women are often faced with choices that seem inevitably to involve personal sacrifices. But I think that you have other choices as well—ways in which marriage, education, and motherhood can be combined, ways in which your husband can share the responsibilities that woman have traditionally taken on.

Client: My husband is cruel to me. When he gets mad he hits me, and yet later he says that he is sorry and ashamed. I don't know why he is like that . . . or how to make him stop.

Counselor: You don't deserve that kind of abuse; no woman deserves to be hit. Many men think they have a right to hit their wives: They say that their wives provoke them and if their wives behaved differently they would stop. And large segments of society agree with that. But that is all nonsense! You can't control or change your husband (only he can do that), but you can make changes in your own life, and I can help you with that.

Client: My mother keeps nagging at me to be a good girl, a respectable daughter, but I don't want to fit into her mold or be like her.

Counselor: It is difficult to establish a new life-style, especially one that conflicts with traditional values. It can make for conflict with parents and others in authority. As a feminist, I can appreciate your struggle and can work with you in exploring options and different ways of resolving the conflicts that you face.

The appropriateness of declaring or advertising oneself as a feminist counselor depends on the counseling setting, the type of clientele served, and the degree of choice clients have in selecting a counselor. Ideally, feminist counselors work in clearly identified feminist counseling agencies, serving clients with well-informed notions of feminism and with a wide range of alternate counseling services available to them. This ideal, however, is rarely the case.

Clients are likely to have misconceptions of feminism. They may have little real choice in the selection of counseling services or have little inclination to search out alternate sources of counseling. A definitive declaration of feminism as a counseling approach, therefore, may be deleterious without an accompanying opportunity for appropriate explication. On a college campus, a clearly labeled feminist counseling service may well be appropriate. In a family service agency serving uneducated and racially divergent groups, a feminist label is likely to be misconstrued. While a feminist analysis applies equally to clients in both settings, the initial presentation and explication of the service will vary. Feminist counselors do not hide or disguise their feminist perspective, but they do use tact and judgment in its presentation, keeping in mind the client's ability to understand and utilize this perspective in her particular situation.

The beginning phase of counseling, therefore, consists of the establishment of a facilitative client-counselor relationship, a full exploration of client problems promoted by counselor attending skills, and the communication to the client of the counselor's feminist perspective. The counselor's orientation to feminist analysis becomes clear to the client and thus makes a distinct impact on the counseling even at this initial stage. This impact, however, becomes considerably more intense in the work or change-oriented phase of counseling.

THE WORK PHASE

The work or change-oriented phase of feminist counseling consists of several unique feminist skills as well as other skills modified to promote feminist goals. All these skills are combined to form a unique feminist counseling constellation. The change-oriented skills of feminist counseling are the most distinct aspect of this counseling approach. These skills distinguish the work phase of feminist counseling more perceptibly from other approaches than do the skills of the beginning and termination phases.

Not only are the skills of the work phase different, but the way in which they are exercised is different as well. Feminist counselors deliberately and actively promote a unique social perspective. They frequently take on a teaching or reeducative role in relation to their clients. Counseling, therefore, becomes a more active process, and the level of counselor activity rises higher than in other, more passively reflective, counseling approaches.

In addition, feminist counseling is oriented to the present, and its focus is on the client's immediate situation and the ways in which modifications can be made currently to reduce distress. While feminist counseling recognizes that the past has relevance to a client's present attitudes, feelings, and behaviors and that knowledge of this past can illuminate the present, it does not accept an understanding of the past as a substitute for present action. The focus in feminist counseling remains on what can be done here and now to change current attitudes and situations.

This focus on the present is complemented by a concern that is behavioral. Feminist counseling addresses clients' social situations as well as their reactions to them. Alleviation of distress, therefore, frequently requires changes on both the individual and societal levels. Social situations do not change unless some action is taken to change them; hence, feminist counseling not only helps the client to understand her immediate and larger social contexts but also urges her to act concretely towards changing those contexts, at least the immediate ones. Insight or understanding of causation is not considered sufficient in feminist counseling. Success is instead defined as observable change. Such change can be minute—for example, a client refusing an overburdening request or taking some time and resources to meet an unfulfilled need of her own; on the other hand, conscious actions may very well produce large-scale changes in her life situation. In any case, the object is to promote such behavior changes as indicate that clients are increasingly taking charge of their lives, that they are taking action rather than simply reacting to the behaviors and actions of others.

This concern with the behavioral reduces the emphasis placed on affect, common to other counseling methods. The affective components of clients' problems are certainly recognized and allowed expression in feminist counseling, but they are not allowed to dictate the course of counseling. Clients are encouraged to learn that behavior that does not initially "feel right" may simply indicate inexperience and unfamiliarity with that behavior. Clients' feelings are seen in feminist counseling both as determinants and as products of behavior.

Counselors, as well as clients, may sometimes find this emphasis on active behavior change more challenging than the orientation to the passive gain in insights that marks traditional counseling modes. Counselors who have been trained in traditional approaches to counseling may initially find the transition to a more active counseling style somewhat uncomfortable. However, just as their clients can learn new and more effective modes of behavior, so can counselors acquire facility and finesse with new counseling behaviors through repetition.

FEMINIST SKILLS OF CHANGE PROMOTION

Feminist counseling aims to increase women's independence, autonomy, and personal effectiveness. It recognizes that to reach those goals, changes must be made in social situations and in internalized social prescriptions, as well as in individual psychological dynamics. Feminist counseling skills have been developed to make those changes most effectively and to reach those goals. Each skill has a specified corresponding goal and demonstrates a particular aspect of change promotion as explained below.

Positive Evaluation of Women

The positive evaluation of women is the counseling skill of conveying to the client that she has strengths and attributes developed by virtue of her gender and sex role socialization that have enabled her to cope with demeaning and stressful life situations; these strengths and attributes are to be valued in spite of and contrary to a social system that devalues them.

Women frequently present themselves for counseling with a self-image composed of negative attributes. They see themselves as inadequate in social functioning, at fault in unhappy relationships, and incompetent in tasks associated with achievements. Before being able to take positive change action, they need to regain a sense of adequacy and competence. A feminist counselor can assist clients to achieve this by recounting the accomplishments evident in their female sphere of influence and demonstrating the valuable contributions that they have made.

Many women who seek counseling have a history of sexual oppression and discrimination in employment situations, domestic situations, the legal system, the economic sphere, and other areas of their lives. The hardiness and endurance of women in the face of these tribulations is indeed remarkable. Counselors and clients can profit from taking time to recount a client's accomplishments, to recognize her inherent strengths, and to mobilize these strengths as bases for future change.

To acquire the skill of positive evaluation of women, a counselor must first become aware of the prevailing societal tendency to devalue women, be convinced that this is irrational and unjust, and then personally reevaluate women's traits and contributions positively. Female traits such as affiliation, nurturance, and compassion are increasingly being recognized as essential in effective management of interpersonal relationships. Women have long been experts in these areas. Women's traditional functions of homemaking and child care are essential to the maintenance of societal functioning, and yet these functions have never been accorded the importance they deserve.

These are traits, then, that must be positively valued by the counselor herself. In valuing them, the counselor does not suggest that these define the totality of female functioning. The position she takes is, rather, that since women possess such valuable abilities they have a potential for further personal development that stretches as far as their imaginations.

Social Analysis

Social analysis is the skill, chiefly, of assessing social and cultural restraints that impinge internally and externally on a client's behavior and of helping a client recognize these restraints. Part of the skill lies also in using this assessment to help clients cognitively restructure their world.

Frequently, clients will tell the counselor that their difficulties are entirely self-imposed. Traditional counseling often supports this self-perception by emphasizing unconscious motivation and other intrapsychic dynamics as causes of actions and attitudes.

In contrast, the counseling skill of social analysis highlights the social restraints that contribute to the problematic situation. Many of these social restraints may indeed be internalized, as the client incorporates social norms and standards of feminine behavior. Clients may be active in limiting their options and choices as they rule out those perceived to be masculine, unsuitable for women, or too difficult for a woman to master. This process of choice limitation may not even reach the client's awareness, as she simply follows social prescriptions of female role behavior. Most women are well socialized into submissive, passive social roles. Their quick speech, frequent smiling, allowing of interruptions, fostering of male leadership, avoidance of decision making, and failure to exercise power are behaviors that unwittingly reinforce women's subordinate position.

The feminist counselor uses social analysis to trace the client's problems with internal restrictions to social causes. Clients are thereby helped to understand how their behaviors have been molded, their ideas and standards influenced, and their perceptions of the world shaped by social forces. Once they recognize such forces, clients can begin to acquire perceptions and behaviors that protect them against manipulation by those forces.

Social analysis, therefore, places the focus of counseling outside the client as well as within the client. It encourages clients to take personal action as well as to consider group or social action. Social analysis identifies the individual client's difficulties with those of women as a group and stresses the commonality of women.

Encouragement of Total Development

The skill of encouraging total development is one by which the counselor directs clients by identification, reinforcement, and mobilization of available resources to attend to their total being and to develop every aspect of personality that might increase their personal effectiveness. The goal of this counseling skill is the development or enhancement of androgynous behavior, that is, behavior resulting from the integration of both male and female traits in an individual in a balanced fashion. That is the ultimate goal, but, first, clients must be encouraged to attend to themselves, to explore their own needs, wants, and desires without necessarily referencing them or restricting them to the approval of others. Before a woman can become androgynous in her attitudes and actions, she must first feel entitled to spend time and attention on herself, must feel the legitimacy of attending to her own needs, must feel the right to look after herself in the face of conflicting demands from others.

Many women seek counseling with the stated goal of improving or developing those aspects of themselves which will make them more pleasing to others, or they say that their current distress and unhappiness is somehow related to their inability to please others sufficiently. Alternatively, they may be angry and frustrated that their constant efforts to please others have yielded few personal rewards, and they may want to increase others' appreciation of their efforts. All of these complaints have in common the client's neglect of herself and expectation that her efforts on behalf of others should yield reciprocal gratifications, thereby obviating the necessity of self-care. Women need to be disabused of these notions and encouraged to tend to themselves first and foremost.

Since women have been socialized to be passive and receptive and since women who attend to themselves are frequently characterized by derogatory terms such as *demanding, pushy,* and *self-centered*, it is not surprising that considerable counseling time and effort may need to be expended to reach this initial goal of self-attending.

Once a client has recognized the legitimacy of her self-attending, she can be encouraged to direct her development in directions hitherto neglected. It is now that the counselor can urge her to develop and express repressed and unlearned traits typically more characteristic of the opposite sex. This *androgynous counseling*, to use Pyke's (1980) term, helps the client to be more masterful and competent in a greater variety of situations.

By encouraging the client's total development, therefore, a feminist counselor legitimizes the client's self-attending, encourages an active approach to skill attainment and development, enlarges the client's potential behavioral repertoire, and increases the flexibility of her responses. Clients, as a result, will feel and be more competent and be freed of the self-effacing task of constantly pleasing others.

Behavior Feedback

Behavior feedback is the counseling skill of providing clients with accurate and concise feedback regarding their behavior or behavioral manifestations of feelings. It is a skill that requires clear and unambiguous communication by the counselor, communication that may be easily understood and verified by the client. It is communication based on what is seen and heard rather than inferred, construed, or suggested.

Many clients expect elaborate and complex explanations for their behavior, explanations based on unconscious motivation, infantile psychosexual development, or intricate psychological mechanisms. They expect counselors to be experts, to be able to tell them things about themselves that they could not be expected to know or understand by themselves. Counselors are perceived as experts who can interpret the hidden meanings of daily behaviors.

Client expectations of this nature have particular significance for women. If counselors are regarded as experts and as providers of intrapsychic interpretations, clients can then be passive recipients or consumers with no responsibility for direction or self-assertion in the interaction. Clients are thereby absolved of self-scrutiny, of analysis of behavior patterns, and of the arduous task of changing habitual patterns and learning new skills. In short, the client role in such interactions parallels the traditional passive female role that lay at the root of the distress in the first place.

By using the skill of behavior feedback, a counselor can circumvent the destructive pattern described above and encourage a more active and direct participation by the client in the counseling. By refusing to be an expert, the counselor demands more of the client in terms of input and involvement. By relying on observations rather than interpretations in her feedback, the counselor encourages the client to verify or refute observations. Counselors using behavior feedback aim for a dialogue between themselves and their clients as equal participants, through which the client may gain greater self-awareness and the counselor a greater understanding of women's reality.

The skill of behavior feedback, therefore, promotes an egalitarian client-counselor relationship, encourages the active and total participation of clients in the counseling encounter, and explodes the supposed mystique of the counseling process by making it an experience readily understandable by all.

Self-disclosure

The skill of self-disclosure is the counselor's ability to share relevant personal material about herself with the client, with the purpose of furthering the client's counseling goals. Self-disclosure generally takes the form of a self-reference that evaluates or describes oneself or expresses one's personal emotional reactions.

Clients presenting themselves for counseling frequently find it difficult to disclose intimate personal details. The counselor's self-disclosure can encourage the client's self-exploration, and this is the rationale many counseling approaches use in endorsing self-disclosure. In feminist counseling, self-disclosure has several different purposes. Thomas (1977) notes the importance of self-disclosure by feminist counselors in fostering a sense of unity or community between women. By self-disclosure, counselors can demonstrate their vulnerability to the same oppression, the same restictions and subjugation, that clients have experienced. This sense of a common history can strengthen and deepen the counseling relationship between counselor and client.

Rohrbaugh (1979) describes how self-disclosure reduces the covert bias in counseling as feminist counselors clearly disclose their values and philosophical positions. Feminist counselors explicitly acknowledge their position regarding women's status in society, their belief that low status is detrimental to psychological well-being, and their goal of increasing women's power and authority. Counselors make these disclosures so that clients are fully aware of the nature of the counseling process and the direction it will take, so that they can make informed choices about their subsequent counseling participation.

Rohrbaugh also describes how self-disclosure can serve as a source of modeling for the client. By sharing personal experiences related to the client's situation, a counselor can suggest means of coping based on her own experience. This is particularly important in nontraditional areas, where not many role models currently exist.

Pyke (1980) has suggested that the counselor's self-disclosure can also serve to attenuate the power differential between counselor and client. This is particularly important for women who tend to perceive their counselors as authority figures. A counselor who shares her own vulnerabilities and limitations thereby demonstrates her fallability and her commonality with the client. Furthermore, the counselor's disclosures of weaknesses or faults may encourage the client to accept her own limitations in a more positive manner.

Self-disclosure by counselors, therefore, can aid in clarifying the counseling process, in deepening the counseling relationship, in stressing the commonality of women, and in placing the client's limitations in a more positive light. Self-disclosures by counselors require considerable sensitivity in terms of timing, depth, and appropriateness. Such sensitivity is, obviously, not easy to achieve but worth developing, for self-disclosure can be extremely powerful in the counseling encounter when skillfully used.

Skill Interactions

None of the skills described here in itself defines feminist counseling, nor are all the skills necessarily unique to feminist counseling. What is unique is the constellation of skills, their avowed feminist purpose, and their interaction in the counseling encounter, which gives feminist counseling its special character. The net result of skill interactions is a counseling mode that is active, direct, externally oriented, present focused, behaviorally oriented, and egalitarian.

The core skills of feminist counseling work together to heighten the uniqueness or distinctiveness of the feminist counseling approach. Innumerable skill interactions are possible in counseling responses to client statements. Although counselors can learn and understand the skills individually and sequentially, in the counseling encounter the skills become merged and integrated into complex responses reflecting a counselor's personal style.

The following example demonstrates skill interactions in a counselor's response:

Client: I feel terrible at being dismissed from my job. I was just beginning to feel confident in my ability to handle it.

Counselor: I had a similar experience in losing my first job and being totally devastated by it. It's important to remember, however, that this job loss is not necessarily a reflection of your ability or performance. Women tend to be last hired and first fired. Employers still think of women working only for pin money or luxuries. If it is possible that you have experienced discrimination, there are several avenues you can pursue.

The skills of self-disclosure, social analysis, positive evaluation of women, and encouragement of total development can be integrated into a response that not only provides clients with some understanding of their situation but also suggests a course of action to consider. As the individual skills are considered in detail in turn, it will become clear how the skills are integrated to provide a powerful counseling response.

In any learning enterprise, learning the individual components of the discipline is a precondition of mastering the total discipline. Therefore, a consideration of individual counseling components or skills follows.

Chapter 4

POSITIVE EVALUATION OF WOMEN

THE SKILL DEFINED

The positive evaluation of women is the counseling skill of conveying to clients that they have attributes and abilities that are unjustly devalued by themselves and by the society in which they live. Positive evaluation rests on the counselor's ability to communicate to clients her conviction that female attributes and abilities are significant and important.

Using this skill, the counselor not only endorses the positive attributes of clients but also encourages them to revise their bases of evaluating themselves and other women. Counselors assist clients to recognize that their negative self-image is not simply a product of negative interpersonal experiences but also a product of the socially prevalent negative evaluation of women.

The positive evaluation of women is achieved by encouraging clients to view the world from a female rather than male perspective. It helps clients to search out and affirm the value of those qualities that are generally considered to be feminine and of biological functions such as pregnancy, birthing, and lactation. The skill is aimed at reappraising female roles while repudiating the stereotyping of women as the passive sex, unsuitable for authoritative roles.

The positive evaluation of women aims at improving women's evaluations of their own selves and of women in general. It also shows women that such appraisals run counter to larger social judgments. Counselors must, therefore, convey not only a strong positive message that contradicts the history of negative messages about women but also the conviction that these positive messages are right and appropriate even though prevailing social attitudes may suggest the contrary.

LEVELS OF POSITIVE EVALUATION OF WOMEN

Positive evaluation can be conveyed by the counselor to the client at several different levels. The skill level attained at a given moment of counseling may be determined either by the counselor's ability to convey the evaluation or by the counselor's assessment of the client's readiness to react to a specific skill intensity. Although skill levels form an unbroken but graded continuum rather than a series of separate steps, they are presented here as discrete levels simply for convenience of discussion. A scale for the measurement of the skill of positive evaluation of women is presented near the end of the chapter.

The lowest level of the skill is characterized by neutral or negative feedback that gives no indication of a counselor's evaluation of women or even of the specific client. Positive evaluation is totally lacking.

At the next level the counselor begins to evaluate client strengths positively and to indicate that these are common attributes shared by women. Counselors can indicate that the many physically and psychologically taxing functions that women carry out routinely, such as child care, homemaking, and creation of a supportive and positive psychological milieu, are ones that deserve credit and pride and reflect numerous skills, abilities, and competencies. The counseling skill at this level is parallel to a general supportive skill or the reflection of positive regard.

At the third level, the positive evaluation of women is introduced as a notion that is contrary to prevailing social norms of valuation. The client, at this level, is introduced to the idea that women may follow criteria for self-evaluation that may be contrary to prevailing standards but are no less valid and, in fact, are perhaps more so. The client is therefore encouraged to begin developing an evaluation system of her own that is more compatible with women's world view.

At the fourth level of the skill, the counselor articulates the connection between the individual woman's low self-evaluation and the low status of women in society. The client is therefore provided with a cognitive framework in which to develop a new evaluation system and is further provided with a social perspective that complements the newly developing personal perspective. The client at this level is encouraged to enlarge her perspective on her own problems and to see that her negative self-image reflects the usual low evaluation of women. The connection between the personal and the social is clearly made.

At the highest level of the skill, the counselor supplements the client's awareness of discrimination against women with the encouragement of social or common action by women. At this level, the counselor promotes sharing between women, common support between women, and consideration of group action by women. The counselor indicates to the client the difficulty of making a stand alone and the effectiveness of establishing networks of women's supportive resources.

The particular level of positive evaluation that a counselor selects at any given point in the counseling encounter depends on a number of factors. The stage of development of the counseling relationship is one of the factors. The client's personal orientation to herself and to women generally will also help to set the counselor's level of skill. And, lastly, the counselor's own awareness, commitment, and ability to communicate the skill will determine the level of the positive evaluation.

The personal orientation of the client often determines how the skill of positive evaluation is applied by the counselor. A client from a very traditional background, or one from a background of firmly entrenched patriarchy, may require a more gradual introduction to a new system of evaluating women than a client from a more androgynous background. The client's milieu and availability of support also need to be considered in opening a positive perspective. If a positive evaluation of women can be fostered through nothing but the counseling process, then that process clearly has to be more prolonged than when a positive perspective is also offered by other social influences. Women require considerable support in maintaining a positive self-perspective, and the greater the availability of such support in the community, the more rapidly a counselor can increase the intensity of the positive evaluation of women skill.

Finally, the level on which the skill is exercised reflects the counselor's personal awareness, commitment, and ability to communicate her conviction of the validity of the evaluation. A counselor first needs to be aware that her own evaluations have been influenced by negative stereotypes and therefore are in need of continual reappraisal. A counselor must herself be convinced that her client's difficulties must be seen in the context of larger social issues, and she must be able to communicate this awareness to the client. Her skill in positively evaluating her client may, therefore, rise to higher levels as she gains greater awareness of the influence of social forces upon her client and as she learns better to communicate this awareness to the client.

The particular level on which this skill is exercised can be monitored according to the positive evaluation of women scale presented near the end of this chapter. In addition, how the skill generally contributes to the counseling process and its outcome may be assessed.

SUPPORTING RESEARCH

The positive evaluation of women has not been specifically identified in the literature of counseling as a counseling skill, nor has it been studied in relation to counseling outcome. Although in a general sense feminist counseling is founded on such evaluation, positive evaluation of women has not so far been seen as a set of counseling behaviors that can be identified, learned, and empirically evaluated in relation to counseling outcome. Consequently, no research has directly addressed the skill of positive evaluation.

However, indirect empirical validation is available in several different forms. Client feedback from a feminist counseling service, for example, indicated that one of the most helpful products of this service was the discovery of the centrality, helpfulness, and competence of women. The positive evaluation of women had clearly been communicated by the counselors providing this service, and this was found to be personally helpful by the clients receiving this service (Johnson, 1976).

Another indirect confirmation of the relationship of positive evaluation of women to successful counseling outcome is derived from research demonstrating how positive evaluation affects clients' low self-esteem. Several studies have demonstrated that individuals with chronic low self-esteem respond positively to positive evaluation (Holstein, Goldstein & Bem, 1971; Milburn, Bell & Koeski, 1970). Women, simply because they are women, suffer from chronic low self-esteem in comparison to males.

The previously cited studies on self-esteem enhancement have indicated that positive feedback needs to be consistent and repeated in order to enhance self-esteem. This is particularly necessary for the positive evaluation of women because it is not socially reinforced. Only through consistent repetition can a positive evaluation counteract the long history of negative evaluation. From the studies on self-esteem, then, the feminist counselor may perceive the need to reiterate her positive evaluation of women over a sustained period and to consistently demonstrate her conviction about the validity of such evaluations.

As this brief review indicates, the skill of positively evaluating women has at present only indirect support from research. Studies on self-esteem have amply demonstrated its importance in enabling women to take charge of their lives, and this research indicates, at least by implication, the value of positive evaluation as a tool of feminist counseling.

REQUIREMENTS FOR SKILL ACQUISITION

A feminist counselor may acquire the skill of positive evaluation in three different ways. First, she must raise her own awareness of the many ways in which women are devalued. At the same time, the counselor must herself be convinced of the injustice and irrationality of such devaluation. Lastly, she must increase her ability to communicate her awareness and conviction to her clients. As each of these areas represents different phases of skill acquisition, each will be discussed in turn.

Awareness

The activities, traits, and accomplishments of men and women are often differentially valued simply on the basis of sex, and a critical examination of the bases of these differential evaluations is the first step in developing counselor awareness of negative female evaluation. Male activities are generally regarded as superior to female activities even when the nature of the activity itself does not vary. This differential evaluation goes so far that even the terms used for activities may vary according to gender. For example, women preparing meals are *cooks*, while men preparing equivalent meals are *chefs*; women performing basic hospital functions are *nurses' aides*, whereas men performing similar functions are *orderlies* (significantly *not* aides to nurses).

Statements of fact or opinion will frequently be differentially valued depending on the gender of the speaker. Golberg (1968) demonstrated that an essay ascribed to a male writer was consistently rated higher than the identical essay ascribed to a female writer. This differential evaluation came from both male and female raters. This same discrimination is frequently seen in everyday conversation: A woman makes a statement that is ignored only to have the same statement reiterated a few minutes later by a man, who is accorded attention and deference.

Similarly, affective responses will often be differentially evaluated depending on the actor's gender. Women who react angrily, for example, will frequently elicit responses to the emotional state rather than the precipitating cause. They will be labeled as *overreactive, volatile,* or *lacking in control,* and responses will be placating or soothing ones. Men, on the other hand, who react angrily tend to elicit reactions that remedy the cause of the anger, the affective response being regarded as an appropriate reaction to the misdemeanor.

Ambitions, expectations, and future plans will be likewise regarded differentially dependent on whether they are voiced by men or women. Men's plans and ambitions are generally regarded as serious and feasible, whereas women's ambitions tend to be dismissed as unrealistic and unlikely, especially when there is a potential conflict with motherhood or wifely duties.

Counselors who have been brought up in a society that devalues female accomplishments, female cognitions, female affective reactions, and female aspirations cannot expect to have totally escaped from this influence. They must, therefore, be prepared to examine continually and repeatedly their evaluations of female clients. Are clients diminished in any way becaue they are female? Is less expected of clients because they are "only women"? Is less respect accorded to female than to male clients? These questions and others in a similar vein bear reiteration to ensure that counselors provide clients with sustained positive regard.

Counselors also need to examine the ways in which they may be failing to acknowledge the positive traits and characteristics of womanhood exhibited by their female clients. Women, for example, have generally developed a high sensitivity to the emotional reactions, nonverbal communications, and unspoken motivations of others. This trait, to some extent, has been developed by virtue of women's subjugation to, and necessity of appeasing, dominant male forces in their lives. Nevertheless, this sensitivity and awareness of others is a valuable human relations skill. Its importance is increasingly being recognized in the commercial and industrial spheres in addition to the more commonly recognized family or home spheres.

While sensitivity to others is a valuable trait on which women need to pride themselves, women also need to be alerted to the drawbacks of overdependence on this trait. Overdependence on sensitivity to others can impel some women to assume responsibility for the total emotional comfort and security of others. These women need to be made aware that although they have skills to promote a positive affective milieu, they do not have the responsibility to ensure everyone's happiness. Sensitivity to others can also promote a reactive rather than active stance in women and can preclude women's self-attending and self-expression. Lastly, an expectation of reciprocity frequently accompanies this sensitivity, an expectation that is more often frustrated than fulfilled. Counselors, therefore, while valuing female sensitivity, need to alert their clients to the dangers of heightened responsibility for others, passivity and self-neglect, and unrealistic expectations of automatic reciprocity that may accompany such sensitivity.

Domestic and home management skills are also possessed but devalued by most women. Little recognition is given by women or by society as a whole to the range and complexity of skills that constitute traditional homemaking. Many of these skills are transferable to settings outside the home and frequently are given considerably more value there. It is to help women value these abilities that a counselor can use the skill of positive evaluation.

In summary, traditional traits and characteristics of womanhood deserve to be valued. A counselor needs to be aware of and to acknowledge and value these traits in her clients before she can expect them to progress in counseling. Furthermore, by urging a positive evaluation of female characteristics, women can increase their impact on the social order. Women with pride in their contributions in the past and present can more readily develop ways to influence the future. A counselor who has an awareness of the strengths of her clients can work with this strength and can use it as a foundation for further growth and development. In mutually valuing these traits, counselor and client alike can put a greater value upon womanhood and women's role in society.

Conviction

A counselor must not only be aware of the need for the positive evaluation of women but must also be convinced of its validity, importance, and relevance to a client's situation. In assessing the client's situation, the counselor needs the ability not only to recognize low self-evaluation but also to be convinced of its relationship to low evaluation of women. Only if the counselor is convinced of the primacy of this explanation over alternate explanations (for example, childhood experiences) is it likely that positive evaluation and the feminist perspective will be communicated to the client.

Communication

The counselor's awareness of and conviction about the positive evaluation of women are only effective when they can be adequately communicated to clients. Communication is most effective when it is in easily understood language that clearly demonstrates the relevance of the issue to the client's immediate situation. For example, a middle-aged woman who finds herself suddenly alone with limited resources for self-support is not likely to benefit from a political discourse on employment discrimination but will almost surely benefit from an inventory of her traits and abilities that have enabled her to cope in the past. The direct approach to positive evaluation, nevertheless, needs to be done with sensitivity to the client's position. Overemphasizing the positive can appear to be insincere and/or ingratiating. Concrete demonstrations of the benefits of particular traits or abilities are the likeliest ways to restore or increase women's confidence and self-esteem.

The timing and relevance of positive evaluations also need careful assessment by counselors. Clients in crisis or experiencing considerable distress clearly need to deal with precipitating factors before considering the more long-range actions addressed by a positive evaluation. Anger and frustration frequently result when the client finds herself continually assessed negatively by others. Some expression may have to be given to these feelings before the client can be receptive to positive evaluations. Clients, overwhelmed by negative evaluations, may need some time before they can accept the validity of the counselor's positive evaluations and see the benefits of positive self-evaluations and self-appreciations.

The skill of communicating a positive evaluation of women to clients can be improved by repeated practice. Even counselors with an active feminist consciousness may initially find it difficult to communicate that consciousness to clients in simple, direct statements. Role-playing exercises are a valuable method of rehearsal and experimentation with a variety of responses to select those that best suit each individual counselor. Studying clinical transcripts of other feminist counselors can also offer suggestions to individual counselors as to how their own responses might be modified or strengthened.

For this purpose, a clinical situation is presented here with three different counseling responses demonstrating the skill of positive evaluation of women. Role-playing exercises follow, which provide the opportunity for skill practice, and transcripts of the exercises can be used for comparing student's role playing with that of experienced feminist counselors. A scale is provided for assessing the level of demonstrated counseling skill.

CLINICAL EXAMPLES

The clinical examples and selected counselor responses presented here are synopses of real cases that have been condensed for presentation. Several feminist counselors provided responses to these client situations in clinical simulations. These counseling responses are provided to demonstrate the range of responses that is possible in applying a particular counseling skill. Learning counselors are encouraged to explore and experiment with innovative expressions of skills rather than simply reiterating model statements. Comments follow each counselor response to highlight and summarize counselor intent.

The Case of Brenda Smith

Brenda was a thirty-three-year-old married homemaker, mother of three children aged thirteen, eleven, and seven. She sought counseling because she was experiencing intermittent periods of crying and lethargy alternating with periods of anxiety and compulsive domestic activity. Although she described her husband as supportive and her children as well-adjusted, she stated that she found no positive gratification in her domestic role and was increasingly feeling incompetent and ineffective.

Brenda: I wish I didn't feel so incompetent. When I was younger I felt like I was bright and able to do everything—but now I don't feel like I'm fit for anything!

Counselor A: You have mentioned that you're managing your home, participating in the school co-op, involved in the church, and raising three kids. That sounds like you are doing a lot of things and doing them well. What you do takes a lot of thinking, a lot of organizing, and a lot of planning. I think that you have many skills and accomplishments for which you don't give yourself credit.
Comment: The counseling response in this case is a cataloguing and demonstration of the number of skills and abilities that are involved in the client's everyday activities. The counselor is encouraging the client to reevaluate her accomplishments to increase her appreciation and pride in what she has done.

Counselor B: Well, you've certainly been very active in doing things with your kids, participating in their lives to make them more pleasant and interesting. That kind of volunteer effort receives very little credit . . . certainly not the credit it deserves. If a mother does it, it is "just busy work"; if a teacher's aide does it, it's called "professional involvement."

Comment: Counselor B demonstrates that it is not the instrinsic value of the activity that determines its social value but rather the status of the individual performing it. Just a mother doing a job is not nearly as important as a person who does a task as part of her paid employment.

Counselor C: Well, Brenda, it seems like what you've been doing are things that are more important for others than for yourself. You haven't felt that you were developing as a person even though you were performing very valuable activities for your family. Perhaps now is the time to consider doing some things that would make you feel like a growing and developing person.

Comment: Counselor C is demonstrating that although the client's activities are valuable, they are not serving to enhance the client. Without diminishing the importance of what she has been doing, the counselor is suggesting that she explore more personally satisfying activities.

Counselors in the three examples above were promoting a positive evaluation of women in their responses to the client. They were not denigrating the traditional activities in which the client was involved, but they were redirecting her to evaluate them in a different fashion. They were anticipating that through this reevaluation the client would be able to increase her self-esteem and more vigorously pursue her self-development.

Certainly the examples above do not constitute the entire range of counseling responses that could be used to convey a positive evaluation of women to clients. They simply represent a small sample of ways in which three counselors have practiced this skill.

The role-playing exercises that follow provide student counselors with an opportunity to practice the skill of positive evaluation of women. Each exercise given here presents a specific problem. The student counselor can compare her own responses with those of experienced feminist counselors, provided in the transcripts that follow. This comparison should be aimed at considering possible modifications rather than emulating a prescribed feminist counseling response.

ROLE-PLAYING EXERCISES

Role Play #1

Client: I feel like I am completely taken for granted. What I do at home is not noticed until it is left undone. My teenage children expect me to do their chores, but they never show me any appreciation.
Counselor:

Role Play #2

Client: I am going on a weekend trip with a group of friends who are witty, talented people. I feel so inferior in that group because there is nothing I can contribute to it. I always end up feeling like an outsider.
Counselor:

Role Play #3

Client: Quite often during the day I start thinking about some little thing that is bothering me and start to cry. I can't get on with my work, and I feel so silly.
Counselor:

Role-playing exercises are most effective in learning new counseling skills when they are accompanied by feedback and remediation. Feedback, to be accurate, should be provided by an audiotape or videotape. An accompanying critique by an experienced counselor can provide further suggestions for modifying the response in subsequent remedial role playing. In the absence of experienced counselors or peers to provide the critique, the learning counselor can compare her performance to counseling transcripts of the kind given here. The critiquing process, whether initiated by the counselor herself or others, should ideally be followed by remedial practice wherein the suggestions offered by the critique can be assimilated.

In providing critiques of the role-playing exercises for the skill of positive evaluation of women, the following considerations should be addressed:

1. Did the counselor help the client feel that she possessed traits, characteristics, and accomplishments of value, or did she diminish the client by accepting the prevailing low self-evaluation?
2. Did the counselor connect the client's specific distress with the common situation of women?
3. Were the counselor's statements convincing as she encouraged the client to evaluate her own and/or women's accomplishments more positively?
4. Were the counselor's statements clear, direct, and easily understandable? Did she avoid jargon and ambiguous terminology?
5. Were the counselor's statement relevant to the client's immediate problems, or was the counselor pursuing a seemingly irrelevant feminist agenda?

ROLE-PLAYING TRANSCRIPTS

Upon completing the role playing and receiving some feedback about it, it is useful for counselors to compare their own performance with that of an experienced feminist counselor. The following transcripts are therefore presented for the purpose of making such comparisons. Counselors should bear in mind that these transcripts represent only a sample of the variety of ways in which positive evaluation of women could be expressed. It is frequently useful to extract elements from more experienced counselors' approaches to augment one's own, but any given counselor must finally develop a counseling style that is best suited to her personally. The following transcripts include many responses demonstrating the skill of positive evaluation of women that might be of value in a counselor's repertoire.

Transcript of Role Play #1

Client: I feel like I am completely taken for granted. What I do at home is not noticed until it is left undone. My teenage children expect me to do their chores, but they never show me any appreciation.

Counselor: It sounds like you do a lot at home, but it does not give you much satisfaction. What do you think would give you more satisfaction? Do you want more recognition from your family, or would you simply prefer to be doing something else?

Client: I do such a lot! And it makes me angry that no one even notices it. Even my husband just hides behind a newspaper when he comes home and shows no interest in what I've been doing.

Counselor: Sounds like it's not just a matter of appreciation . . . sounds like you feel you're not even noticed, and that no one cares about you.

Client: That's true. Sometimes I feel like there is not much point in going on from day to day.

Counselor: Well, you're not alone in feeling that way. A lot of women at home find that what they do is unappreciated and unnoticed. It is a very distressing feeling, especially considering the time and effort that you put into it. But you can make it better by deciding what it is you want and then doing something to achieve that.

Client: I want them to notice me more and to realize what I am doing for them.

Counselor: Well, then you will have to tell them that.

Client: But I shouldn't have to tell them. I'm always looking out for their feelings. I always praise what they do without being asked to do that. I let them know how much I care for them. They don't have to ask . . . I just do it.

Counselor: I believe that you do that, and I'll bet that you are very good at it, too. Women are well trained to be attentive and responsive to the feelings of others, but men and children don't generally have that sort of training. They need to be told that you need some appreciation and attention. There is nothing wrong with asking . . . it doesn't diminish the value of the appreciation just because you asked for it.

Client: But if they really cared about me they would see how unhappy I am, and they would do something about it.

Counselor: You know, I'll bet that your family has very little inkling how unhappy you are. They see you as super-efficient

Mom, always on the go, always managing everything, always managing to make life a bit better for the family. They probably think of you as a strong, capable person and don't stop to consider that you have needs of your own.

Client: I guess that's true. I don't like the family to see me feeling upset, so I always pretend to be happy with what I'm doing. I try not to complain because I don't like to sound like a nag.

Counselor: So your family doesn't really know what it is costing you to do everything for them. They don't realize what it takes out of you, what is demanded from you.

Client: No, I guess I make it all look so easy and effortless, like I'm enjoying it all the time. Perhaps that's why they don't feel it is necessary to express any appreciation.

Counselor: That may certainly be part of it. Also expressing gratitude is something of a habit that needs to be developed. You can encourage them to develop such a habit.

Client: That might be something to try.

Transcript of Role Play #2

Client: I am going on a weekend trip with a group of friends who are witty, talented people. I feel so inferior in that group because there is nothing I can contribute to it. I always end up feeling like an outsider.

Counselor: Well, that really is a useful thing to consider. What can you add to the group that will make you feel like a part of it?

Client: I don't know. I can't sing or play the guitar. I can't even tell jokes.

Counselor: What about some of the more practical things? What about helping to organize the food or helping with the housekeeping?

Client: Well . . . yes, I could do some of those things.

Counselor: But, you're thinking that that's not as good as singing or making music or telling jokes?

Client: Well, yes.

Counselor: But isn't it true that on weekend outings one of the things people look forward to most is the meals? You're an excellent cook; you could make up one of your special dishes. Or do you think that food is unimportant?

Client: Of course food is important.

Counselor: Sure it's important, and you know what else is important? — The fact that you're doing something, that you are joining in with the group, that you are contributing something to it. You might not be the center of attention, but you are doing something to increase your sense of belonging to that group.

Client: Yes, I guess by doing some of those things, I would be helping out.

Counselor: I think you will find that anything you do, whether it be cooking or just helping with chores, will increase your sense of group membership.

Client: I guess I could volunteer to help with the food.

Transcript of Role Play #3

Client: Quite often during the day I start thinking about some little thing that is bothering me and start to cry. I can't get on with my work, and I feel so silly.

Counselor: Well, it's not unusual to get upset over little things when you have major problems as well. The little things might just be indicators of a bigger problem that you have.

Client: Well, I don't know. My problems all seem so trivial. My husband says that I am concerned with nothing but trivia.

Counselor: I guess that makes you feel pretty insignificant, when your concerns are dismissed as trivial.

Client: Well, yes. What I think about is pretty important to me, but he doesn't seem to think so.

Counselor: Well, what women find important is not always regarded as important by men. Generally, the things that women value are not given the importance they deserve. They are important! If it's important to you, then it is important.

Client: And when he criticizes me, I just start crying. Then he gets madder and doesn't listen to me at all.

Counselor: Crying is often a response to frustration. It sounds like your husband doesn't realize how much of your time and effort goes into looking after those little things that he dismisses as trivial.

Client: He doesn't know because he doesn't want to listen to me talk about them.

Counselor: Well, clearly he doesn't have the same degree of involvement with your concerns as you do. It may not be reasonable to expect him to share all your interests and concerns. However, when you feel something is important and he should be involved, you may need to tell him that very clearly.

Client: I don't think he would listen.

Counselor: Well, if you made a point of telling him at an appropriate time and indicating that this was very important, I expect that he would listen.

Client: I'm not sure . . .

Counselor: You know, I suspect that your husband doesn't realize that when he dismisses your concerns as trivial, he is discounting you as a person. I don't think he means to belittle you; he simply isn't aware of the effects of his comments.

Client: You're right about that. He doesn't think about what he says to other people.

Counselor: The important thing is that you realize that your concerns are valid and deserving of attention. If your husband can help you with them, then talk to him. If he's not involved, perhaps you can talk to someone else.

Client: I guess that's why I'm here.

MEASUREMENT OF POSITIVE EVALUATION OF WOMEN

Scales for the measurement of each of the feminist counseling skills have been developed (Russell, 1982). These scales were first tested by rating the transcripts of responses by experienced counselors to a videotape of a simulated client making ten typical client statements. Several independent raters were used for each scale to obtain measures of interrater reliability. The rating on each scale indicated the overall level of counselor performance on that scale. Although these scales were used primarily as research instruments, they can also be used as guides for counselors wishing to monitor their performance on a particular skill. The scales can be used, for example, to rate performance on role-playing exercises and to serve as another source of feedback to aid in remediating the performance.

The Positive Evaluation of Women Scale measures a counselor's skill in communicating positive regard for the client as a woman in a society in which female traits and behaviors are devalued. The scale measures the extent to which a counselor is able to communicate her conviction that a client possesses traits and attributes that deserve positive evaluation and that their present low evaluation represents the low evaluation of women generally.

This scale ranges from the lowest level, at which counselors do not express any values regarding women and fail to provide clients with any positive feedback whatsoever. The second level presents responses that are positive in a general fashion, and the third level includes reference to the general low social evaluation of women. The fourth level measures clear support of women's traits, and the fifth level measures the explication of the connection between the low self-evaluation of the individual and social evaluations of women.

The levels of this scale are differentiated primarily on the basis of an increasingly explicit positive evaluation of women in the context of a sexist society. What the skill measures is, thus, the counselor's skill in articulating this positive evaluation of women.

POSITIVE EVALUATION OF WOMEN SCALE

Level I

The counselor does not reveal her attitude or values toward women generally or to the client in particular. The counselor does not respond with any statements that describe the client in a positive fashion.

Key Words: *No positive evaluation*

Level II

The counselor makes general supportive statements that refer to client strengths but not to client gender. The counselor draws parallels between the client's situation and women generally but does so only to demonstrate the commonality of experience.

Key Words: *General supportive statements*

Level III

The counselor makes one positive response to the client that indicates that she is valuing traits or characteristics commonly not accorded value. An oblique reference to women's inferior status is made.

Key Words: *Beginning support of women's traits*

Level IV

The counselor makes two positive responses regarding client attributes and adds the observation that client distress is related to women's low status.

Key Words: *Clear positive evaluations*

Level V

The counselor values positively the client's attributes in two or more statements, indicates the social origins of low evaluations, and urges the client to develop alternate evaluation standards based on a female perspective.

Key Words: *Social positive reevaluation.*

CLINICAL APPLICATIONS

The skill of positive evaluation of women is useful in addressing both individual feelings of inadequacy on the part of clients and their general sense of inferiority as women. Both of these types of feelings are frequently reinforced or supported by significant others in their lives and by prevailing negative stereotypes of women. Women frequently accept these negative evaluations and devalue their accomplishments, take a subordinate role in relationships, and relegate as unimportant their concerns and anxieties.

When seeking counseling, many women complain of a lack of appreciation or valuation by others. This, however, is generally coupled with their personal lack of conviction that they and their accomplishments are worthy of positive evaluation.

To address this lack, a counselor using the skill of positive evaluation of women begins by encouraging clients to develop a sense of their own worth, of appreciating and valuing who they are and what they do. Before women can expect to be valued by others, they have to have some conviction about their own value. Only with a personal sense of positive value can confirmation from others be sought.

A counselor's skill in using positive evaluation rests largely on her awareness of the myriad manifestations of negative female evaluation in everyday interactions. This awareness, when coupled with a conviction that negative evaluations of women are unjust and irrational, can be used to encourage a new framework of client evaluations. Direct and simple communication of these evaluations facilitates client assimilation of such values.

The positive evaluation of women is basically a supportive skill and as such has application in all situations in which clients need support and encouragement. It is more than simple support, however, in that it explains through a feminist analysis of society the prevailing low valuation of women. As such, this skill is firmly grounded in feminist philosophy.

The positive evaluation of women is, therefore, a basic and fundamental counseling skill that reflects the counselor's feminist philosophy and forms the basis of her feminist approach to clients. Since it is supported and buttressed by an analytical knowledge of the social context that provides the rationale for the present low status of women in society, social analysis is another important skill of the feminist counselor. This, then, is the next skill considered here. Whereas the positive evaluation of women introduces some basic tenets of the feminist philosophy, social analysis expounds and develops them for the benefit of clients.

Chapter 5

THE SKILL OF SOCIAL ANALYSIS

THE SKILL DEFINED

Social analysis is the counseling skill of assessing social and cultural restraints impinging internally and externally on clients. The skill includes the use of this assessment in assisting clients to restructure cognitively their world through recognition of social influences. David (1980) has described social analysis as a process in which counselors assist clients to gain a cognitive understanding of the psychological oppression of women. This understanding enables women to perceive that they have been enjoined to learn and engage in behaviors that help others to succeed while they themselves forgo actions that would increase their own effectiveness as autonomous individuals. Rawlings and Carter (1977) have referred to this same process as *sex role analysis*. Thomas (1977) reports that the majority of feminist counselors subscribe to this counseling technique in that they engage in some form of consciousness raising.

The skill of social analysis is, therefore, very similar to the process of consciousness raising. The primary difference between the two is that social analysis is part of a client-counselor interaction rather than a shared experience between a group of women. Although consciousness-raising groups were not primarily intended to be therapeutic, the process of analyzing problems in terms of individual and social factors clearly offers participants therapeutic benefits in the form of shared understanding, mutual support, and identification with the commonality of women (Brodsky, 1973; Kravetz, 1976). In individual counseling, this interaction, support, and identification are admittedly limited to that between client and counselor but are nevertheless extremely beneficial for the client involved.

The skill of social analysis assists counselors to redefine the distress of their clients as an expected and normal reaction to the conflicting and unrealistic demands to which they are subject. In seeking counseling, many women regard their psychological distress as a sickness, an abnormality, an internal disorder requiring an internal remedy. Women frequently feel that they are to blame for their distress, that their own inadequacies have resulted in their despair, and that their weaknesses have precipitated their problems. A feminist counselor, using the skill of social analysis, enables clients to recognize the social component of their problems and see their deficiences as the results of socialization and restricted opportunities rather than as individual faults.

Social analysis in counseling promotes the transition from a personal to a political perspective by providing an explanation of the low status of women, an indication of how this low status affects individual women, and a commentary on the common experience of all women. Social analysis, therefore, provides a rationale, that is, a cognitive framework, for the skill of positive evaluation of women, discussed earlier. The explanations offered by a social analysis can serve to mitigate the sense of self-blame and self-abnegation experienced by many clients. By providing a broader perspective, a counselor can assist her clients to cope more effectively with their problems.

Social analysis also allows clients to assess realistically the social barriers that still exist to thwart their personal development as women. Sexual discrimination is still rampant, in the forms both of direct and overt restrictions that bar women from various roles and associations and of indirect and covert restrictions that reinforce traditional roles and discourage deviations from them. Social analysis in counseling allows a consideration of these barriers as well as of alternate ways to overcome such barriers. In some cases, the tactics may be direct and confrontal; in others, a more gradual and conciliatory approach may be deemed more effective. Clients always have the choice regarding both the type and range of action they wish to take against perceived barriers.

Social action is clearly recognized as a necessary counterpart of social analysis, but the timing and the type of such action is not prescribed. Many clients simply do not have the resources to participate in social action at the time of counseling but may nevertheless benefit from the knowledge that such action is possible and likely to be effective some time in the future. Other clients may be anxious to unite with other women in similar situations to exert power to improve their common lot. Social action is generally a long-term goal, once the alleviation of personal distress has been accomplished.

Social analysis, although a cognitive skill, can also be used to explain and improve women's affective responses to situations. Clients frequently report feelings of hopelessness, powerlessness, and helplessness in response to problematic situations, which are perceived as overwhelming. Social analysis can demonstrate that such feelings are partly the result of female socialization, which fosters the image of the helpless female, and partly the result of restricted opportunities to develop various coping skills. Social analysis, therefore, not only can demonstrate that feelings or emotional reactions reflect conditioning rather than personal inadequacies but can indicate the direction for potential remediation. Self-condemnation and self-blame leading to introspective spirals of decreasing hope are thereby avoided.

Social analysis can generate strong emotional reactions in clients. As social analysis identifies social barriers that thwart women's total function, as it reveals the resultant bias and skew in women's development, as it indicates the powerless position of women, it can generate considerable feelings of resentment and anger. Feelings of self-blame that clients previously experienced may be transformed into anger at powerful others. While this mobilization of anger may be a positive force if channeled into producing change, it can also be detrimental if it is simply expelled against persons close to the client. Counselors using the skill of social analysis are most effective when they emphasize the social context of oppression or discrimination. Clients may well feel that the responsibility for such oppression rests with their intimates, who are therefore legitimate targets of anger, but it is becoming increasingly evident that such simple expressions of anger are not necessarily therapeutic in the long run. Anger expressed against individuals can precipitate retaliation and escalation of the original conflict. Counselors must ideally help clients to turn that anger to socially applicable action.

The skill of social analysis, therefore, requires a counselor to be sensitive to her client's ability to understand and act upon the restructured social perception that is offered. The social analysis needs to be one that fits the client's needs and capacities rather than one that reflects the current level of awareness of the counselor.

LEVELS OF SOCIAL ANALYSIS

The skill of social analysis can be expressed at several different levels. The determinants of the level of skill displayed at any moment in counseling include client characteristics, the phase of the counseling process, and counselor ability.

The lowest level of the social analysis skill in fact reflects an absence of a social perspective and an exclusive focus on intrapsychic client dynamics. At the next level, there is a recognition of external forces influencing the client's situation. Counselors at this level acknowledge external factors as potentially relevant in the client's currently distressed state but, nevertheless, insist that the changes to be made must be totally internal. Counselors here acknowledge environmental or social pressures impinging on clients but recommend a remedy through adjustment to these forces rather than external change.

At the third level, counselors address both internal psychological processes and external determinants of clients' problems. Clients are encouraged to address both components equally. External forces that are elucidated by counselors at this level may include sex role socialization and sex role stereotyping.

At the fourth level, counselors not only focus equally on internal and external forces but clearly enunciate the connections between these two sources of restraint. Social analysis at this level assists clients to perceive the relationship between their specific difficulties and the problems of women in general. At the highest level of social analysis, counselors explicate not only the internal and external connections but also the political or social forces that lead to sexual discrimination. The need for collective political action is therefore implied if not directly addressed.

In using social analysis, like any other counseling skill, the needs and capacities of the client must be the foremost consideration in determining the level of skill application. An older, traditional woman is less likely to benefit from a full-blown feminist analysis in the first counseling encounter than a young, liberal woman. A traditional woman may require a more gradual introduction to a feminist analysis, an introduction that emphasizes the rapidly changing expectations of women. This approach does not invalidate her previous role performance but rather places it in the context of a changing social system. On the contrary, a young woman who is searching for a female identity and role model may be quite receptive to an intense social analysis in the first encounter. Numerous client characteristics, therefore, such as age, education, previous exposure to a feminist analysis, and degree of commitment to traditional sex roles, all may be important factors to consider when using social analysis with clients.

Social analysis also becomes more appropriate as progress is made through the several phases of the counseling process. In the beginning phase of counseling, when the focus is on assessment, social analysis will be relevant in directing the scope of the assessment. Social analysis helps counselors to identify clearly both the external and internal forces impinging on a client's situation. However, this phase is not appropriate for the full explication of these social forces.

In the work or action phase of counseling, once the initial exploration has been completed, counselors are likely to find social analysis extremely beneficial in assisting their clients to understand their situations and to chart avenues of change.

In the termination or ending phase of counseling, too, social analysis may become a significant part of the counseling process. Since collective action, as well as individual action, is a goal of social analysis, the termination of counseling may include some possible collective action for both client and counselor to pursue. However, this again will depend on the characteristics of both the client and the counselor involved.

SUPPORTING RESEARCH

Social analysis has not yet been defined in the counseling literature as a specific counseling skill and hence no direct research evidence exists to support its effectiveness in counseling. However, several indirect sources of evidence cumulatively give credence to the potential effectiveness of this counseling skill.

Feminist counseling outcome studies give some indications of the effectiveness of a social analysis. Johnson (1976) reports in her study of twenty-four feminist therapy clients that aspects of their counseling rated most helpful included gaining awareness of a universal female experience that had been shared by counselor and client alike. It was important for these clients to realize not only that their difficulties were shared with other distressed women but also that apparently strong and capable women were likewise subject to similar discrimination and subjugation. The social analysis not only provided a perspective but also provided hope for the successful resolution of dilemmas.

Marecek, Kravetz, and Finn (1979) compared the outcome of the feminist counseling of 201 women with that of the traditional counseling of 207 different women. Women who identified themselves as feminist or radical very clearly found traditional counseling less effective than feminist counseling. It can be inferred that the social analyses of these radical women conflicted with those of their traditional counselors and thus thwarted positive counseling gains. Clients with some feminist awareness, therefore, are likely to reject the social analyses of traditional counselors or be dissatisfied with the lack of any evident social analysis in the counseling process. The importance of social analysis is suggested even more strongly by the fact that traditional women found feminist counseling just as helpful as, if not more helpful than, traditional counseling. The social analysis presented by feminist counselors to traditional women, therefore, was not rejected, although perhaps not perceived by traditional women to be as important as it was by radical clients. It should be noted, however, that in this study, even the traditional women had already been participants in consciousness-raising groups and hence had some familiarity with feminist philosophy.

Studies in consciousness-raising outcomes offer further support for the effectiveness of social analysis. Kravetz's (1980) review of such studies concluded that a consistently positive response to exercises in social awareness was found among previous participants in such groups. Reports of significant psychological changes and behavioral changes include findings of increased self-esteem, increased awareness of social impact on women's lives, increased awareness of commonality and solidarity with other women, and social role changes both within the home and outside. These reported changes are all consistent with the aims and goals of social analysis. Social analysis, in counseling as in consciousness-raising groups, is likely to have similarly beneficial outcomes.

A comparison of consciousness-raising groups and self-help groups to peer-counseling groups for widows, by Barrett (1978), found that the consciousness-raising groups were most effective in bringing about positive life changes. Furthermore, this approach received the most positive ratings of helpfulness and educational value from the clients. Not only was the social analysis informative, but it also promoted specific changes in behavior and life circumstances.

Although the evidence of consciousness-raising efforts highly supports the effectiveness of social analysis, its relevance is limited by the fact that group processes rather than individual counseling processes were investigated. These reports, therefore, must be regarded as tentative evidence for the effectiveness of social analysis, and their conclusions must await confirmation from studies of the individual process.

REQUIREMENTS FOR SKILL ACQUISITION

Awareness

Counselors using the skill of social analysis must first of all enhance their own consciousness about women's social status and its relation to individual women's distress. In the early days of the Women's Movement, feminist counselors were able to monitor their own awareness through organized consciousness-raising groups. As the popularity of such groups diminished and the feminist consciousness filtered down to the general populace, alternate avenues have opened towards maintaining and developing counselors' feminist awareness.

Nevertheless, women's groups, even when they are not primarily devoted to consciousness raising, have remained a strong platform for sharing feelings, analyzing similarities and differences of life experiences, and supporting mutual efforts. Women's networks, women's peer groups, and various professional women's groups form such platforms, which both heighten women's awareness and also encourage collective action.

Recent sociological literature, both popular and academic, is another source for increasing awareness of women's social condition. Publications that deal with the subject of counseling women, although not necessarily all feminist, certainly reflect an awareness of sexist biases in social interactions. The strong social analysis that now characterizes the social sciences and humanities has significantly increased the awareness of gender differences in social perception and experience. Counselors can dramatically heighten their awareness of social factors affecting women by searching this literature.

The influence of experienced feminist counselors and feminists active in social causes can also serve to increase the awareness of less experienced counselors. Female academics, politicians, and professionals and women with long involvement in the Women's Movement are visible sources of inspiration and support for less experienced women. These more experienced women willingly lend support to those with less experience as the need for a prolonged and sustained campaign to promote women's causes becomes evident.

Conviction

A counselor may be aware that women are systematically discriminated against and oppressed socially but may not see the relevance of that social analysis to the counseling encounter. There are at least two reasons that may account for this. The first is that the counselor may experience and understand the oppression on a personal level but not see its relevance to clients who may be in very different situations. A counselor may need to deepen and broaden her social analysis to gain a conviction about its relevance to her clients as well as herself. A second reason for lack of conviction about the importance of social analysis in counseling may relate to the professional training of the counselor. Counselors trained in traditional intrapsychic orientations may find it difficult to incorporate externally based social analysis. Conviction can be increased by a more thorough understanding of the goals of social analysis as well as by observing its effectiveness in action. A counselor must be convinced of the relevance of social analysis to a client's situation to be able to communicate it effectively.

Communication

The communication of a social analysis can range from elaborate discussion of historical antecedents and sustaining political forces that perpetuate the subjugation of women to a simple analytic statement that demonstrates for a particular woman her subjugation based on her sex. A counselor's effectiveness in communicating a social analysis can be improved by considering several factors.

Communication requires that sufficient information be conveyed to clients so that they may restructure their cognitions and devise a concept of their situation that is different from the one currently held. Counselors, therefore, may find that their level of participation is increased, that they are providing more than customary amounts of input, and that their statements are more rational-persuasive than reflective.

The active communication of a particular social and political perspective to clients presents an ethical dilemma for some counselors. These counselors maintain that a neutral position in counseling is the best. However, at the same time, these counselors regularly provide intrapsychic interpretations that are highly authoritarian and reflect a particular bias that is frequently inimical to women. A dialogue between counselors and clients concerning their respective ideas about the social order is less likely to be directive and authoritarian than intrapsychic interpretations that clients have no choice but to accept.

Communication of social analysis is most effective when it is presented in simple terms that suit the client's ability to assimilate the information. Some examples of simple communications are as follows:

> *To a depressed homemaker:* Since housework is an unpaid task, many women feel that what they do and who they are, are basically worthless.
>
> *To an intimidated young woman:* You've probably been told that speaking up for your rights is being pushy or bossy, but it is possible to be assertive in a positive way.
>
> *To a dissatisfied wife:* Most women grow up with the expectation of being rescued or fulfilled by the "right man." It's hard to give up that expectation as unrealistic and take on the responsibility for your own happiness.

More complex statements are clearly appropriate for more sophisticated clients who are well informed about the feminist philosophy. However, care must nevertheless be taken that relevance is not sacrificed in applying abstract or more loosely worded rhetoric. Academic and philosophical arguments are important in the women's movement, but with individual clients the focus must always remain on the individual and her situation.

The communication of a social analysis, therefore, involves the active participation of a counselor who must offer simple and direct statements to her client, statements that enable the client to gain a different understanding of her situation. This communication is a skill readily mastered by counselors and one that can be refined by repeated practice.

CLINICAL EXAMPLES

The following example is a summary and synopsis of an actual clinical case. Following the brief description and presentation of a typical client statement, three feminist counselors provide their responses. Each response demonstrates a different way of using the skill of social analysis. A comment follows each response to elucidate the counselor's intent.

The Case of Doreen Black

Doreen was a forty-five-year-old woman, separated from her husband, living alone in an apartment in a large, metropolitan city. Doreen had separated from her husband a year prior to seeking counseling. During this time her three adult children had been helpful and supportive, but after helping her cope with the initially confusing matters of finance, legal rights, and housing, the children expected Doreen to be less dependent on them. As a consequence, Doreen was feeling abandoned, fearful of being alone, and distressed about a future that she perceived as bleak and desolate. Doreen had been a secretary before her marriage but had not worked for over twenty years.

Doreen: Now on top of all my other problems, I have to worry about getting a job. I'm not qualified to do any kind of work, and just the thought of looking for work is absolutely petrifying. Offices today are so complicated with computers and new machines. I could never learn to use them.

Counselor A: Right now I'm sure that you feel scared. Any kind of new experience is pretty frightening. Most women like yourself never expected to have·to go back to work. Marriage provided a social slot for you, and your whole life was determined by that position. Now that you are no longer a wife, your social world might seem to hold no place for you. But there are many other ways of looking at that world and placing yourself in it. That is what we can work on together.

Comment: Counselor A is using social analysis to provide a different perspective on the feelings of fear and anxiety experienced by the client. This different perspective is designed to give hope to the client and provide some direction for future action.

Counselor B: Well, Doreen, I agree that trying to get a job can be a pretty tough proposition, especially when some employers discriminate against older women. However, that kind of discrimination is not legal, and other employers are aware of the benefits of maturity in their employees. We can work together on looking for all the positive things you can offer an employer and plan how you can best present this.

Comment: Counselor B is using social analysis to indicate that sexist and age-linked discrimination does exist, that the client may need to be prepared for it, and that this is inherently not only unfair but invalid. The counselor is encouraging the client to combat such attitudes by clearly enunciating the positive claims that refute them. Individual action is proposed at this stage, but conceivably social action might be contemplated at a later point in the counseling process.

Counselor C: Well, it's true that offices today are increasingly mechanized and computerized. A lot of women find computers frightening, but in reality operating one requires little more skill than operating a complex stove or sewing machine. You don't have to know how a computer works to operate it, any more than you have to understand how your stove works to boil water. Women used to be discouraged from driving cars because of their lack of mechanical knowledge. That turned out to be a lot of nonsense, and the same is true of computers today.

Comment: Counselor C is using social analysis to demonstrate that the client has been socialized to exclude herself from certain areas because of supposed deficits in ability to handle them. The counselor indicates that such suppositions are invalid and that the client has demonstrated by her previous experience that she is capable of mastering tasks such as computer operations.

These three examples of social analysis show the many different ways it can be used to combat women's negative self-image and to provide a different perspective on their situation. Each example suggests a different way in which the client could reassess the difficulties presented on both internal and external levels and shows how these difficulties might prohibit effective personal functioning.

In none of the above examples did the counselors engage in debates about feminist philosophy or the women's movement. Rather, they presented simple statements about the commonality of women's social position, about the negative effects of female sex role socialization, and about current barriers that still restrict female development. These simple statements enabled the client to see the connection between her situation and the situation of women generally. Likewise, they also provided some indication of necessary actions to be taken. Clearly, then, such simple and direct statements are most likely to be beneficial for clients.

Many counselors engaged in counseling women may be quite familiar with feminist philosophy but less so with the practice of translating this into simple clinical statements. The following role-playing exercises are designed to provide the opportunity to respond with simple social analysis statements.

ROLE-PLAYING EXERCISES

Role Play #1

Client: My husband just died four months ago and left me with a house mortgage, a car loan, and other bills that I know nothing about. He took care of all those things when he was alive. There is no one to do this anymore, and I feel so stupid.
Counselor:

Role Play #2

Client: I want to be a better wife and mother so that my children and husband will be happier. I want so much to make them happy.
Counselor:

Role Play #3

Client: I quit my office job a while ago, so I could devote more time to my painting. But my husband thinks I should be able to prepare gourmet meals, mind the kids, and keep the house spotless and to do my painting in my spare time.
Counselor:

To be of maximum benefit, role playing should include feedback and remedial practice. Ideally, the procedure that was described in relation to the role-playing exercises in the previous chapter should be followed. The recommended steps, in summary, are:

1. Two participants should alternate playing the roles of counselor and client.
2. Role playing should be recorded on audio- or videotape.

3. A critique of the tape should follow each role play, preferably by a more experienced feminist counselor.
4. Transcripts of feminist counselors enacting roles should be reviewed.
5. Role play modifications should be considered on the basis of the critique and the modeled role plays.
6. This feedback should be followed by remedial role playing.

In this process of commenting on the role playing, the following considerations should be addressed:

1. Did the counselor communicate to the client that her experience reflected women's common status?
2. Did the counselor explain that the client's problems were the result of both social forces and psychological processes?
3. Did the counselor indicate that sexual discrimination still exists and that social remedies are necessary?
4. Did the counselor communicate in a form that suited the client's ability to understand?
5. Did the counselor clearly and directly relate the social analysis to the client's individual problems?
6. Did the counselor promote a new and different understanding or perception of the world by the client?

These questions can serve as guidelines for the individual critiques of the role-playing exercises. Another source of feedback that can aid in forming the critique is a modeled response by an experienced counselor. Such modeled responses follow in the transcripts below.

ROLE-PLAYING TRANSCRIPTS

The following transcripts provide examples of how experienced feminist counselors performed the role-playing exercises presented earlier in this chapter. The transcripts are provided as examples, not as prescriptions of how social analysis should be used. Social analysis is used by each counselor in a way this is compatible with her style and her client assessment. Transcripts can best be used to garner suggestions and ideas that can be incorporated into the personal style of each counselor.

Transcript of Role Play #1

Client: My husband just died four months ago and left me with a house mortgage, a car loan, and other bills that I know nothing about. He took care of all those things when he was alive. There is no one to do this anymore, and I feel so stupid.

Counselor: It all feels pretty overwhelming doesn't it?

Client: Yes, he took care of everything when he was alive. I didn't do any of it.

Counselor: That's not unusual for women. You know that, don't you? Most of us just don't learn about money and finances and things like that.

Client: I never even thought about those kinds of things.

Counselor: So are you trying to take it all on yourself now?

Client: Well, there's no one else to do it any more. All these bills are coming in, and I don't know where to start. I just feel so stupid!

Counselor: It can get you pretty panicky to start with.

Client: I get so angry with myself. How could I have been so stupid! Why didn't I pay attention to this stuff before? It's just like I was living in a bubble.

Counselor: That's right. That's the way most women are kept. Why should you have been any different? And it does make you feel dumb when you come out the other end.

Client: That's me, all right.

Counselor: And it's like you're starting where other people started at age twelve or fifteen, and that's probably the age you feel when you're trying to deal with those things. No wonder you feel dumb!

Client: I haven't even paid the bills for the funeral. I don't know which accounts to use, which I'm able to use, how to get it out of some of the accounts.

Counselor: Banks can be pretty intimidating, especially for women who have had little experience with them. They tend to be male institutions, but I think they are becoming more sensitive to women's needs. Perhaps you could get one of your friends to go with you the first time, so that you can do it independently later on.

Client: I have some friends who seem to manage on their own, but I would be too embarrassed to ask for help.

Counselor: Embarrassed?

Client: Yes, well, I've let things get into such a mess. My friends are pretty organized. If I tell them how poorly I've done they will really think I'm foolish.

Counselor: Well, handling money is a skill that has to be acquired. You're probably pretty efficient in the kitchen, but that is something that you've learned from years of experience. When you first started cooking you were probably pretty clumsy, but look at you now! Looking after finances will be just like that . . . awkward at first, but better with time.

Client: It just seems so difficult.

Counselor: I expect your friends found it difficult at first, too, but now they're managing fine. I'd encourage you to talk to them.

Client: Yes, I guess I should.

Transcript of Role Play #2

Client: I want to be a better wife and mother so that my children and husband will be happier. I want so much to make them happy.

Counselor: Are they unhappy now?

Client: Well, yes. My husband complains a lot . . . about the house not being tidy, my cooking being bad. And the kids, they are always fighting and squabbling. I should be able to manage things better.

Counselor: And what about you? Are you happy?

Client: No, but if I could make them happier, then I would be happier, too. As it is, I just feel tired, I sleep a lot, and that just makes it all worse.

Counselor: So perhaps your first responsibility is to yourself. If you felt better, you'd probably have more energy to do the things that need to be done.

Client: That's what I want, but I just don't seem to be able to get that extra energy.

Counselor: Well, it could be that you've been like a car that's busy carrying everyone else about but doesn't have fuel for itself. You've been so busy looking after everyone else that you've neglected yourself.

Client: I get so exhausted looking after the kids and trying to please my husband, too. I don't have much time for myself, and even when I do, I don't know what to do.

Counselor: That's a pretty common experience for women. Women tend to be so busy looking after others that they don't take time to think about themselves or what they really want. We're so accustomed to putting others first that we tend to lose touch with ourselves. It might be worthwhile thinking about what would be satisfying for you.

Client: It would satisfy me to see my family happy.

Counselor: True, but that is really out of your control. No matter how hard you try or how hard you work, you cannot ensure happiness for them. Ultimately each person is responsible for her or his own happiness, and that includes you.

Client: Well I know that if I was sure I was doing the best for my family, that would make me happy.

Counselor: Well, again, that's something that you will never know. Each of us does what she can, but you never know if it is the best or if there even *is* a "best." Women frequently expect that they will somehow be rewarded if they are selfless and subservient to their families, but that rarely happens. Your children will go on to develop their own lives; you husband has his life. You need to look after your personal life as well.

Client: I guess that may be so.

Transcript of Role Play #3

Client: I quit my office job a while ago, so I could devote more time to may painting. But my husband thinks I should be able to prepare gourmet meals, mind the kids, and keep the house spotless and to do my painting in my spare time.

Counselor: How did you decide to quit your job? Was it your decision or something your husband wanted?

Client: Oh, we both wanted it. My husband thought it would be good for me to be at home . . . good for the kids. When I worked I was so tired. And I wanted to seriously develop my painting career.

Counselor: Sounds like you had pretty different expectations. He wanted you to be a housewife; you wanted to be a painter.

Client: Well, that may be part of it, but he says that my time is so flexible that I should be able to fit my painting around my housework.

Counselor: In other words, your painting is not really a job or career. It's more of a pastime or hobby?

Client: No, it's a job, but I should be able to do both. But I get frustrated when I'm in the middle of a painting and I have to stop to pick up the kids or get dinner.

Counselor: Sounds to me like you don't take your painting very seriously either. No one else will respect your desire for a career unless you put a priority on your painting and ask others to respect it.

Client: But I should be able to do both. It's just a matter of being organized. When I worked in the office, I still got all my housework done.

Counselor: Maybe that's because your job had priority, and everything less important was fitted in around it. Now the situation is reversed, and the housework has priority.

Client: I guess so, but it's hard to place priority on my painting when my husband shows so little interest in it. I always ask about his work, but he never asks about mine.

Counselor: I'm sure that you make more of an effort to be interested in your husband's work than he in yours. Women generally tend to regard men's activities as important and interesting; they've been trained to do that. Men haven't had the benefit of training about women's activities. Your husband may not even realize how important painting is to you, or he simply may not be able to share your interest. Ultimately your painting may be something that you do mainly for your own satisfaction.

Client: But what is the point of being married if you can't share each other's interests?

Counselor: Marriage certainly involves sharing, but that sharing doesn't have to be all-inclusive. You are both individuals with different interests. Some of your interests you may want to share more with friends or colleagues.

Client: But I make an effort to be interested in his work. He doesn't make an effort to be interested in mine.

Counselor: It may help to tell him that, but you should be prepared to pursue some things independently. You are entitled to a life that is separate from his.

Client: I think I know that, but sometimes it's hard to remember.

MEASUREMENT OF SOCIAL ANALYSIS

Role-playing exercises can be evaluated on the Social Analysis Scale that follows. The scale was designed to measure counselor skill level in transcripts of ten client statements and ten counseling responses. Rising levels of the scale indicate increases in the amount and depth of social analysis.

The Social Analysis Scale measures the counselor's ability to assess the client's presenting problems in terms of both social and psychological factors and to communicate this dual assessment to the client. An underlying internal-external dimension is present in the scale, although at upper scale levels the connection between the internal and external is measured.

The lowest level of the Social Analysis Scale represents a counselor's complete lack of awareness or total disregard of social, environmental, and situational factors in the client's problems. At this level, the counselor is totally focused on intrapsychic dynamics. At the next level, there is some recognition of external forces, but the key to change or remedy lies nevertheless in the intrapsychic domain. At the third level, the counselor pays equal attention to internal and external factors, with some consideration of sex role stereotyping included. At the fourth level, the counselor makes clear the connections between internal and external forces and the role of socialization in perpetuating and reinforcing existing barriers. At the highest level of the scale, the needs for both social change and women's attainment of social power are recognized.

SOCIAL ANALYSIS SCALE

Level I

The counselor perceives the client's problems as individual, possibly arising from psychological conflicts rooted in childhood experiences. The counselor maintains that internal changes must be made so that the client can adjust to prevailing situations. All counselor responses are intrapsychic, and none relate to social, environmental, or situational factors.

Key Words: *Completely intrapsychic*

Level II

The counselor acknowledges external factors but chooses to focus on internal psychological dynamics for remediation. One or two responses include consideration of social, environmental, or situational factors.

Key Words: *External references, internal predominance*

Level III

The counselor recognizes both internal and external determinants of the client's problems and addresses both. Three or more responses include social, environmental, or situational references, and the client is directed to attend to both internal and external factors. Sex role stereotyping may be referred to indirectly.

Key Words: *Equivalent internal-external focus*

Level IV

The counselor alerts the client to the relationship between her specific difficulties and those of women generally. In making the three or more external references, the counselor elucidates the connections between these and internal processes.

Key Words: *Connections to women's situation*

Level V

Women's low social evaluation and lack of power are included in the consideration of the internal-external connections and the three or more references to external factors. The need for social action in conjunction with individual change is implied.

Key Words: *Increased social power*

CLINICAL APPLICATIONS

Social analysis in counseling assists clients in gaining a different perspective on their problems, one that points out that women's predicaments are products of social constraints and internalizations of sex role limitations as well as of personal dynamics.

Women frequently seek counseling because they feel that they are personally and totally responsible for their misfortunes. These feelings of self-blame and guilt are frequently reinforced by traditional counseling, which treats distress as a manifestation of individual pathology. Social analysis places the focus of counseling on the interrelationship of internal and external factors.

Social analysis is a consciousness-raising experience wherein counselors enable clients to link their individual situations to women's social status in general. Fostering an alternate recognition of individual situations is one goal of social analysis, and fostering long-range social change is another.

Social analysis can be presented at different levels of intensity or depth depending on client characteristics, phase of counseling, and counselor skill. Ultimately the intensity of the social analysis depends on the client's needs. It is unlikely that a reflection of differential status related to gender will be foreign to even the most traditional clients. The awareness of the injustice of such discrimination, however, may vary considerably. Rationalizations based on women's lesser abilities, capacities, and inherent worth have been internalized by many women as justifications for discrimination and oppression of women.

Counselors engaged in social analysis need to be aware of the support networks that are available to clients who begin to challenge female subjugation. Social analyses that pit individual women against the prevailing totalitarian forces of oppression can be damaging if supportive sources are not at hand. Individual women may be able to make individual changes, but large-scale social changes require collective action. Counselors must take care to encourage individual change that is feasible and allocate social change to collective actions by women.

In summary, social analysis is a counseling skill that aims to increase the client's understanding of the social forces, including female subjugation, that contribute to individual distress. Although the skill aims at cognitive changes, it is evident that corresponding behavioral changes are desirable. These behavioral changes are more directly addressed by the skill of encouraging total development, outlined in the following chapter. Social analysis, therefore, is a necessary but not sufficient skill to bring about change in a client's life situation. The skill of encouraging total development aims to translate the social analysis into concrete behavioral changes that will benefit the client.

Chapter 6

THE SKILL OF
ENCOURAGING TOTAL DEVELOPMENT

THE SKILL DEFINED

The skill of encouraging total development consists of counselor behaviors that help clients develop all elements of their character that lead to increased effectiveness. These elements include ones previously neglected because they conflicted with sex role stereotypes.

Total development in women has suffered from two restraints of social origin. The first is the depiction of any self-attending by women as selfish or narcissistic. The second is the channeling of female development into stereotypically feminine directions that limit personal effectiveness. The skill of encouraging total development, therefore, consists of remedies to these two problems. First, self-attending and pursuit of personal development are generally encouraged. Secondly, encouragement is particularly focused on those aspects of the self previously neglected or rejected because of their conflict with traditional sex role models.

Feminist counseling literature has tended to emphasize the latter androgynous goal of this skill. Pyke (1980) sees in androgynous counseling the goal of enlarging the clients' cognitive and behavioral response repertoires, which is reached by encouraging the development and expression of repressed and unlearned traits typically more characteristic of the opposite sex. Sturdivant (1980) focuses more on the integrative aspect of this skill, describing the goal as one of integrating emotions with intellect and feelings and intuition with thinking and problem solving.

Androgynous development is clearly the goal of encouraging total development, but reaching that goal requires an initial willingness of clients to attend to themselves. Women seeking counseling frequently exhibit a reluctance toward self-attending, preferring instead to focus on relationships and affiliative behaviors, which they perceive as primary. The counselor must, therefore, encourage self-attending in order to reach androgynous goals.

The encouragement of self-attending and the encouragement of androgynous behaviors are equally important components of the skill of encouraging total development, and each will, therefore, be discussed in turn.

Self-attending

Women seeking counseling are often deficient in self-attending. Their experiences have largely been other directed, focused on meeting the needs of others, pleasing others, being obsequious to others, and sometimes manipulating others in the hopes of achieving some small measure of self-fulfillment. This personal history makes it difficult for the counselor to redirect women to develop their potential as autonomous individuals responsible for their own development and fulfillment.

The counselor frequently finds that her clients have had little opportunity to develop their capacity for self-responsibility. Typically, women simply tend to transfer their dependence from father to husband to son. The expectation that some other person will take responsibility for directing their life frequently remains constant through the life cycle. Socially, there are few rewards for women who focus on themselves and develop clearly independent life-styles. The dependent position of women as auxiliaries or appendages to male figures necessitates attending to the dominant other rather than the self.

Finding themselves in positions of dependence, women sometimes develop indirect modes of self-assertion, such as manipulation. While these modes are only occasionally successful, they protect women from the risk of confrontations. That is why many women prefer these modes over a direct, goal-oriented approach to self-development. Counselors must, therefore, be able to demonstrate to clients that direct actions on behalf of themselves are possible, potentially effective, and likely to be personally satisfying. Although replacing indirect modes of behavior with more direct actions may initially involve some personal risks as well as some social censure, counselors can emphasize the potential for personal growth and enrichment of personal relationships.

Women's self-attending and autonomous functioning are also curbed by the heavy emphasis on other-directed behavior in female socialization and the implicit expectation that attention offered to others will be reciprocated. Replacing the other-directed actions by self-directed ones, therefore, can engender guilt at not meeting socially prescribed responsibilities. Women's past experience has frequently taught them that when other's needs are given precedence, their own needs have to be suppressed. Attending to themselves, therefore, leads to the assumption that others' needs will be neglected and the women will be at fault. Counselors can help clients to overcome the resulting guilt by demonstrating the benefits of egalitarian relationships.

The notion of reciprocity in meeting personal needs is often firmly entrenched in, although not always articulated by, women. The other-directedness of women is not always totaly altruistic but is based on the expectation that some measure of compensation, some measure of reciprocity, will ensue. Women seeking counseling frequently complain of other people's insensitivity to their needs, others' apparent lack of caring for their wishes, and others' disregard of their vulnerabilities. Again, the counseling task of demonstrating that these expectations are unrealistic and that expectations of others must be supplanted by self-responsibility is one that is not always easily accomplished. Projecting responsibility for self-fulfillment onto others, particularly when it accords with notions of simple justice, can be a habit difficult to overcome.

Self-attending in women, therefore, is not only socially discouraged but also likely to engender numerous negative emotional reactions. Guilt is a common reaction as women perceive that self-attending concomitantly results in the neglect of their socially prescribed vocation of caring for others. Despair may arise as the myth of reciprocity inherent in self-abnegation is destroyed and as the unlikelihood of others' meeting these expectations becomes apparent. Fear is a frequent response to the initial realization of the need to assume personal responsibility. Women who lack experience in risk taking can be particularly vulnerable to such fears.

Counselors, therefore, may find the task of encouraging self-attending beset by barriers. These barriers, however, can be overcome with repeated and graduated encouragements that are tailored to client needs and capacities. The benefits of pursuing self-development can be emphasized, especially as the deficits of neglecting such development are generally more than apparent in women's distress and unhappiness.

Androgynous Development

Androgyny is the integration of male and female traits, and androgynous development has been advocated as a counseling goal by numerous feminist counselors (Kaplan, 1977; Rawlings & Carter, 1977; Sturdivant, 1980). In feminist counseling, both male and female traits are valued, and clients are encouraged to develop typically male traits such as assertiveness while using such valuable and typical female traits as compassion and sensitivity.

Androgynous goals are pursued in feminist counseling both on an interpersonal or social level as well as on a practical or skill level. Women's socialization encourages certain interpersonal behaviors that tend to make them less effective while it discourages them from entering areas of valuable practical training. Counselors encouraging androgynous development, therefore, need to address both the interpersonal and practical requirements.

Women's verbal habits in interpersonal relationships frequently undermine the significance of their contributions. Because of their socialization, women generally tend to be tentative, deferential, and hesitant in their statements rather than assertive. Simply encouraging women to speak more forcefully and with more conviction can frequently increase their chance of securing them esteem and respect for their statements. Women who can clearly state what they require from a relationship are much more likely to receive it than those who merely hint or make oblique statements in that regard.

Likewise, nonverbal behaviors by women frequently undermine the intent of their verbal statements and contribute to their subservient status. Constant and obligatory smiling and a deferential posture and gait are all examples of behaviors that indicate submission, an eagerness to please, and a lack of seriousness of purpose. Acquiescence in interpersonal relationships is further communicated by a low voice, by tentativeness of statements, by a rising inflection at statement closings, and by an unwillingness to interrupt others while readily allowing interruptions to oneself. All these behaviors foster and allow domination by others with a concomitant denial of women's equality in relationships.

To encourage androgynous development, a counselor can direct her clients to examine and analyze their interpersonal behavior for these traits of acquiescence and subservience. The counselor can then help clients to replace such behaviors with more assertive and self-assured behaviors that are more likely to win them respect.

Although women can clearly benefit from becoming more assertive and self-assured, frequently there is some hesitation in developing these traits. Women are aware that a change from acquiescence to assertiveness is not always likely to be applauded or rewarded by others. Negative reactions are likely to ensue, and challenges to the balance of power in relationships may have to be faced. These negative reactions can be particularly distressing for women who, as part of their acquiescent demeanor, have developed a high sensitivity to others' reactions. Counseling, therefore, while encouraging assertiveness and so-called masculine behavior in interpersonal relationships, equally needs to prepare clients for potential negative reactions by others.

Clients may also hesitate in developing assertive behaviors because these seem alien and unnatural to them personally. Counselors may need to explain that, as in any new skill acquisition, repeated performance will not only improve the skill but also make it seem more natural and comfortable. Another cause for hesitation may be the secondary gains that are provided by acquiescent and passive behavior. Childlike dependence has the benefit of avoidance of personal responsibility, whereas assertiveness and assuredness require taking responsibility for one's actions. Again, counselors may need to stress the benefits of autonomy, increased personal identity, and increased self-actualization that accrue from a more assertive stance in interpersonal relationships.

The development of practical as well as interpersonal skills is encouraged in feminist counseling. Even today, women are still diverted from acquiring many useful practical skills that would enrich their lives, such as athletic skills, mechanical skills, and mathematical skills. Deficiencies in these skills clearly detract from women's ability to deal effectively with their world. For example, inexperience in financial management is a common reason for women's financial dependence, which can be alleviated only by acquiring the requisite financial skills. The counselor's encouragement in acquiring such a skill is clearly vital in ensuring the client's progress in counseling.

However, the development of practical skills is not an easy undertaking, and counselors encouraging it can expect several kinds of resistance. The first is the client's perception of personal ineptitude in acquiring skills. Female socialization proceeds as effectively as it does because women are taught that their personal failings, their personal inadequacies, preclude them from some areas of activity. Thus, many young women readily exclude themselves from studying mathematics, physics, computer sciences, and other related scientific disciplines because they believe they lack the ability to master them. Feminist counseling, using skills of social analysis and encouragement of total development, seeks to dispel such myths and to encourage positive actions that disprove the myths.

The development of androgynous behaviors also entails taking risks, facing the uncertainty inherent in any new undertaking, particularly one for which social models may be lacking. Unfortunately, female socialization also inhibits risk taking. This inhibition begins in childhood as little girls are enjoined to be cautious and conservative, strengthens through adolescence when conformity to peer expectations tends to preclude experimentation and risk taking, and continues into adulthood when security and stability tend to have greater importance for women than for men. Learning new and different skills, therefore, can be disquieting or even frightening for many women. Counselors need to recognize and validate such reactions before they can be replaced with positive actions for skill acquisition.

The development of new skills, furthermore, can be an arduous task that must be sustained over a considerable period of time and that may necessitate considerable self-discipline and self-denial. Counseling, therefore, needs to assess, enhance, and sustain the motivation level of clients, possibly over long periods.

Counselors encouraging androgynous development in clients can increase their effectiveness in a number of ways. First, by relating androgynous development to social analysis, clients' feelings of personal inadequacy and ineptness can be diminished. Secondly, the negative emotional reactions engendered can be recognized as valid reactions to a new and different experience. Counselors can encourage clients to reevaluate these reactions as feelings of excitement and exhilaration inherent in new adventures. Recollections of childhood experiences wherein new skills were readily and voraciously tackled can be used to draw parallels to the current situation. Thirdly, the seeming arduousness of the task can be diminished by stressing the positive evaluation of women and recounting the many difficult tasks that clients have mastered in the past. Lastly, the long-term nature of many learning tasks can benefit from links with support networks and auxiliary supportive community resources.

This two-phased skill of encouraging total development, therefore, is likely to be beset both by external constraints and negative social sanctions and by internalized restraints reflecting the pervasive sex role socialization of women. Counselors, therefore, may have to keep applying the skill of encouraging total development through prolonged periods and to supplement it with the skills of positive evaluation of women and social analysis. Counselors may also find that the skill can best be sustained with the help of other supportive resources and networks for women.

The ultimate benefits of total development clearly apply not only to clients seeking counseling but to women generally. If women expect to have significant social impact, then they need to acquire the skills necessary to do so. Only when women in numbers have such skills can they more readily move into positions of power and dominance. One hopes that the resultant exercise of female power will promote the status and position of women as a group.

LEVELS OF ENCOURAGING TOTAL DEVELOPMENT

The extent of the counselor's exercise of the skill of encouraging total development can vary with client characteristics, counseling phases, and the ability level of the counselor. Encouraging total development, at its lowest level, is diffuse or directionless. At the next level, the skill is one of encouraging total evelopment as an auxiliary activity rather than as an end in itself. At the third level, self-development is clearly encouraged, and recognition is given to possible perturbing personal reactions as well as to negative reactions from others. At this level, clients are advised of the desirability of self-development but also alerted to the potential emotional turmoil and physical strain that may be entailed.

The next level of encouraging self-development includes sustaining motivation by identifying the positive rewards of such effort along with the negative effects of neglecting personal attending and development. At the highest level of applying the skill of encouragement of total development, the counselor tries to develop both masculine and feminine traits in an integrated personality that allows maximum flexibility and capacity to cope with a variety of situations.

The level of skill depends on client attributes, phase of counseling, and counselor ability. Client attributes will determine whether self-attending or androgynous development should be put first in the counseling encounter. Self-attending needs to be encouraged in those clients with a history of other-directedness and self-neglect. Androgynous development may follow this, or it may be addressed initially with those clients who are primarily debilitated by their overdependence on female traits or deficiency in male traits.

The sequence or phasing of counseling also plays a role in determining the appropriate level of encouragement of total development. Feminist counseling skills, although not by necessity sequential, do have some cumulative benefit, and both positive evaluation of women and social analysis can prepare a foundation for more effective encouragement of total development.

In addition, the level of encouragement of total development reflects the particular counselor's awareness, commitment, and ability to communicate the value and benefits of such development. Some of these benefits have been clearly demonstrated through empirical evaluation of areas related to total development.

THE SUPPORTING RESEARCH

The skill of encouraging total development has not been previously conceptualized as a counseling skill and hence has not been subject directly to empirical investigation. However, its two goals, self-attending and androgynous development, have been investigated, and the results have been positive. The effectiveness of the composite skill, therefore, can be inferred.

One result of encouraging the client's self-attending is an increase in the client's self-exploration, which is a variable that has been used to evaluate counseling outcomes by Truax and others. Increased intensity of client self-exploration has been associated with positive counseling outcomes in numerous studies (Truax & Wargo, 1969; Mitchell et al., 1973; Schauble & Pierce, 1974).

Reviews of the literature on androgyny have reported consistent findings of high positive correlations between androgyny and independence, autonomy, high levels of ego maturity, maturity in moral judgments, optimal cognitive functioning, high creativity, and increased sex role adaptability (Pyke, 1980; Sturdivant, 1980).

Androgynous development would therefore seem to be a highly desirable outcome. However, the results of such correlative studies must be interpreted with caution. Although androgyny may tend to be associated with other positive traits, an increase in androgynous behavior would not necessarily lead to corresponding increases in the aforementioned traits. It is entirely possible that some other factor, such as intelligence, is the mediating factor responsible for the high correlations.

Evaluations of assertiveness training, as a counseling approach that aims to increase androgynous behavior, lend credence to the efficacy of the skill of encouragement of androgynous behavior. Jakubowski's (1977) review of the assertiveness training literature indicates that increased assertiveness or strengthened androgynous behavior can be effective in ameliorating numerous clinical problems of women. For example, various depressive conditions, anxiety states, and substance abuses can at least partially be attributed to deficits in androgynous behaviors.

Evaluative research of more active approaches to helping women change their roles such as employment or preemployment counseling, reported by Hansen and Rapoza (1978), also suggests that by helping women increase their range of practical skills, including the more masculine skills, the counselor helps them to become more effective in general. The more skills that are learned, the greater the degree of androgyny and the greater the effectiveness in dealing with the social reality.

Evaluations of the relationship of androgyny to mental health indicators have been criticized for two shortcomings. The first relates to the nature of the concept of androgyny. A number of studies (Deutsch & Gilbert, 1976; Jones, Chernovetz & Hansson, 1978; Kelly & Worrell, 1977) have found that indicators of mental health are correlated more with masculinity than with androgyny, leading to the suggestion that greater masculinity rather than androgyny is the desirable goal of change. Yet, it would be rash to accept that suggestion uncritically. The high social value placed on male traits as compared to female traits may account for their high association with the positive goal of optimal mental health. Only when female traits are accorded social value and accepted as advantageous for personal functioning could both poles of androgynous functioning be equally indicative of mental health.

The second problem with evaluating androgyny in relation to mental health indicators is that these indicators tend to reflect traditional and stereotyped views of personal functioning. Klein (1976) has suggested that feminist counseling aims for a different outcome and that therefore new indicators of mental health are required.

We may note in passing that feminist counseling is concerned with the encouragement of androgynous behaviors only as an interim step to redefining behaviors so that they are no longer sex linked. Rebecca, Hefner, and Oleshansky (1976) have suggested that a more accurately descriptive goal might be *sex role transcendence*. Such a goal would allow maximum choices and opportunity in roles and behaviors not only for women but for men as well. In view of the considerable individual differences within each gender and in view of the greater need for gender flexibility, such a goal would seem optimal for the future of humankind.

The evidence for the effectiveness of the skill of encouraging total development, therefore, remains tentative. However, the indicators are certainly positive, and the questions that are raised in terms of appropriate criteria for determining counseling success are important for feminist counselors.

REQUIREMENTS FOR SKILL ACQUISITION

To acquire the skill of encouraging total development, counselors must be aware of the need for such development in clients, be convinced of its importance in effective problem resolution, and be able to communicate their awareness and conviction readily to clients. The need for total development in women is dependent to some extent on a social analysis that demonstrates how that development has been skewed and biased in a negative fashion. The desirability of total development is also partly dependent on a positive evaluation of women that demonstrates women's potential to pursue development in any area that they should desire.

Awareness

Counselor awareness of the need for clients to develop themselves totally will in part reflect the intensity of their own social analysis. Counselors who are aware of the social conditioning that reinforces women's other-directedness will be aware of the need to encourage their self-attending. Counselors who are aware of the negative social sanctions that are frequently applied to women's self-attending behavior, such as pejorative labels and accusations of neglect of children, can be more active not only in alerting their clients to these potential consequences but also in discussing strategies of dealing with them.

Counselors whose social analysis has demonstrated the bias in skill acquisition that is reflected in female socialization will be more aware of the need to encourage androgynous behaviors in their clients. Likewise, counselors who have an understanding of the social barriers that prohibit women's total participation in some areas can alert clients to both the potential rewards and the hardships they might face in pursuing certain goals.

The counselor's awareness of the need for total development will also indicate the level of positive evaluation of women that has been achieved. Counselors, like other members of society, have been exposed to prevailing low evaluations of women, which lead to diminished expectations for women. Counselors, therefore, must continually examine their own expectations for client development and search for unrealistic diminution or enhancement of goals based on client gender. Counselors must constantly query whether their counseling goals have been too low because of low expectations of women or too high because of a need to compensate for being a woman. This setting of counseling goals clearly requires continual examination and consideration by client and counselor alike.

Conviction

A counselor's conviction about the desirability of her client's total development arises from her own social awareness and experience and the prevailing situation of the client. Counselors can vary in their evaluation of the impact and importance of women's social and practical skill deficiencies. Counselors themselves, although they have chosen to pursue a career, have chosen one that is not radically different from sex role expectations. Their own experience, therefore, may influence the conviction with which they pursue androgynous development with their clients.

Clients, too, will vary in their receptivity to the idea of pursuing total development, and counselors may need to moderate their own convictions in relation to client needs. A feminist counselor committed to the need for androgynous development may find that some clients are prepared only to be introduced to such ideas, not immediately to act upon them. The counselor's conviction about the importance of total development, therefore, may be moderated according to the life experiences of both counselor and client.

Communication

The level of encouragement of total development attained in counseling will depend on a counselor's ability to communicate her awareness and conviction to the client. Since encouragement is a general supportive skill, it is likely to be found in the repertoires of most counselors. Encouraging total development, however, differs in two aspects from the support afforded in general by counselors. First, it encourages development in a specific direction, and, second, it encourages development that may be met with negative social sanctions.

Supporting a particular direction in personal development may present some difficulty to counselors who believe that their counseling is nondirectional. This belief, however, is more a myth than a reality, as counselors ultimately encourage those behaviors and traits which they believe to be beneficial.

The potential for negative reactions in response to client self-attending and androgynous behavior needs to be clearly addressed. Encouragement of particular behaviors, especially novel behaviors not conforming to female stereotypes, may be essential for client development but should not proceed without discussion of possible consequences. A counselor's enthusiasm for pursuing particular goals may need to be tempered by adequate preparation on the client's part to meet possible negative as well as positive eventualities. Clients can readily become discouraged, overwhelmed, and disillusioned if they are not prepared and supported in their difficult tasks. Communication of encouragement by counselors, therefore, needs to be continuous, constant, and reinforced by a supportive network.

The encouragement of total development, therefore, is a counseling skill similar to the basic skill of client encouragement and client support common to most counseling approaches. It differs, however, in promoting a feminist perspective. This difference can most clearly be illustrated through the presentation of clinical examples.

CLINICAL EXAMPLES

The following example is a synopsis of an actual case that was described and presented to a number of experienced feminist counselors. The client's statements were presented to the counselors, each of whom responded in her own way. The variety of responses is presented here to demonstrate the variety of ways in which the skill of encouraging total self-development can be articulated. No two counselor respond in exactly the same way. However, in spite of the differences in counselor responses, there is a commonality in that all of them communicate encouragement of total development at a high level.

The Case of Karen White

Karen was a twenty-six-year-old single woman who was employed as a sales clerk after dropping out of college in her sophomore year. She still lived at home with her parent, while her two older sisters had married and established their own families.

Karen sought counseling for her general dissatisfaction with life, which was compounded by a mild depression and a very low self-image. Karen was bored with her job but had not taken any action to explore alternative employment. She had been the first person in her family to attend college and had felt a great sense of personal failure when she withdrew. Her family, however, had been continually supportive.

Karen's family background was quite traditional in the sense that her mother and sisters had chosen homemaker roles while their husbands worked outside the home to support the family. Karen had some ambition of choosing an alternate role for herself but was not able to follow through on this plan.

Karen: I feel like a total failure. I'm twenty-six years old, and I don't know where I'm going or what I'm doing. I couldn't handle college because of all the competition, all that scrambling for grades, even though I enjoyed studying. I don't think I'm cut out to be a career woman. They seem so suave and sophisticated. Maybe I should just marry somebody . . . anybody. At least then I would have some direction in my life.

Counselor A: Well, that is what your mother and sisters did, and I expect they are relatively happy. But it seems like you wanted something different in your life. You chose to go to college, to do something different. That can be very difficult; you are exposed to a whole different set of pressures and expectation. But it is possible to learn to deal with those pressures, to learn how to set reasonable goals and expectations for yourself, to learn how to manage a work load so that it is manageable but still offers a challenge. I think it is exciting that you wanted something different for yourself. I would like to work with you in helping to develop your ability to pursue those goals.

Comment: Counselor A is illustrating for the client that she has chosen goals for herself that are nontraditional and hence offer both challenges and exciting opportunities. She is emphasizing that the new direction she has chosen requires new skills and capabilities, which can be learned. She is offering her support in acquiring these new capabilities. Counselor A, therefore, is encouraging the client to pursue androgynous goals and alerting her to some of the difficulties inherent in such a course of action. Self-attending is not specifically addressed but implied in the comparison to the mother and sisters. The client is encouraged to attend to herself as a unique being and not as a duplicate of the other female members of her family.

Counselor B: Well, everyone has to decide for themselves what they want. You may expect that marriage will make you happy, give you some direction, but it's not necessarily so. You have to decide what will be truly satisfying for yourself, not just what will please others or get approval from others. You said you enjoyed studying but didn't like to compete for grades. If the studying is satisfying for you, maybe we can look at ways in which you can pursue what you want without the matter of grades or academic recognition being such an obstacle. The most important issue for us to determine is what is going to be satisfying for you.

Comment: Counselor B is placing greater emphasis on the self-attending. She is indicating to the client that primary or intrinsic satisfaction derives from attending to the self rather than the expectations or demands of others. She is proposing that the client examine the obstacles to meeting her needs, implying that there are likely to be both internal and external obstacles that may need to be surmounted. Counselor B is encouraging total self-development in emphasizing self-attending and reinforcing the client's stated androgynous goals.

Counselor C: Jumping into marriage can be a diversion; it can be a way of avoiding difficult choices, a way of escape, a way of providing some temporary excitement in your life. However, it is probably a better idea to take a good look at all the choices you have available to you rather than taking any precipitous action. You mention having a career; you have educational goals that are incomplete. You may be able to benefit from a more structured approach to assessing your interests and abilities. That can easily be arranged. Personally, you seem to have some difficulties in pursuing what you want. Perhaps some assertiveness training would help you with that. A rational and complete analysis of your capabilities as well as of those areas that need further development can probably provide you with that direction that you feel is lacking.

Comment: Counselor C is encouraging total self-development in the goals that she is endorsing as well as modeling a more androgynous manner of approaching the problem. She is stressing a more rational, more structured approach to the situation, rather than relying on intuition and impulse. This particular response does not address the client's affective state, but presumably the counselor would attend to it at some stage of the counseling process.

The three examples of the encouragement of total self-development skill presented above provide an indication of the variety of ways in which this skill can be expressed. Although the three responses differed from each other considerably, they all stressed self-attending rather than conformity with social conventions or traditional expectations. They all encouraged a development that could be considered nontraditional for women, and they indicated that pursuing such a course of action would be beset with difficulties. They emphasized that acquiring new practical skills or new interpersonal skills was basically a matter of learning rather than a matter of intrinsic personal worth or ability.

The brevity of counselor responses indicates that some issues remained untouched. None of the counselors' responses indicated the desirability of integrating the traditional with the nontraditional, or the female and male, aspects of personal development. This may represent a reaction to this particular client, who appeared to be in danger of losing her own aspirations to the dominating effect of her family's traditional background. On the other hand, it may represent the phase of counseling that was being represented, the integration perhaps being pursued at a later phase of the contact.

Since there is such a variety of ways of expressing both the intensity and the level of the skill of encouraging total development, and since these responses may vary considerably with the client problem presented, it would be instructive here to consider a number of different client presentations in role play. Three role-playing exercises follow, which provide an opportunity both to practice the articulation of the skill and to get some feedback from the recipient of the counseling response.

ROLE-PLAYING EXERCISES

Role Play #1

Client: I'm so afraid I may say something stupid in a conversation, so I just sit back and say nothing.
Counselor:

Role Play #2

Client: When I was younger I felt like I could handle anything. Since being home with the kids, I'm not sure what I could do.
Counselor:

Role Play #3

Client: Since I've been on my own, I feel like my children neglect me and my friends don't come around very often. I feel quite abandoned!
Counselor:

Role playing for the skill of encouraging total development will be of maximal benefit if the feedback to the learner is immediate, complete, and supportively critical. The recommended steps for such role playing are briefly reviewed below:

1. Roles of counselor and client are alternately taken by participants.
2. Audio- or videotape is used to record the role playing.
3. A critique follows the completion of role playing.
4. The relevant transcript is reviewed.
5. Modifications of role plays to incorporate elements of transcripts are considered.

In the process of critically studying the initial role playing for the skill, the participants may find it helpful to ask the following questions.

1. Did the counselor clearly convey to the client the desirability of attending to the self, of considering one's own needs and desires and of acting upon them?
2. Did the counselor indicate that self-attending might conflict with feminine socialization and/or with expectations of significant others?
3. Did the counselor indicate that nontraditional or androgynous goals were potentially more rewarding than traditional or strictly feminine goals?
4. Did the counselor alert the client to both internal and external barriers that may be present in pursuing androgynous goals?
5. Did the counselor emphasize a learning mode rather than psychological manipulation in acquiring new skills and/or behaviors?
6. Did the counselor reinterpret fears and anxieties as normal and expected reactions that can also signify potential excitement and exhilaration?
7. Did the counselor communicate her conviction that androgynous development can lead to maximal individual flexibility and ability to cope with a wide variety of situations?

The above questions provide a guideline for studying the role playing. Additional help may also be found in the counseling transcripts that follow.

ROLE-PLAYING TRANSCRIPTS

These transcripts are examples of responses of experienced feminist counselors in the previously presented role plays. These transcripts should be used as examples, as possible ways in which the situation could be handled, rather than as prescriptions. The specifics of applying the skill of encouraging total development naturally depend on each counselor's individual perceptions, but these transcripts will indicate the broad lines along which the skill is exercised.

A learning counselor may find in these responses elements that suit her own counseling style, but she would be wise to avoid a simple and total repetition of another counselor's responses.

Transcript of Role Play #1

Client: I am so afraid I may say something stupid in a conversation, so I just sit back and say nothing.

Counselor: So, in fact, you count yourself out before you even begin. You don't really give yourself a chance to join the conversation.

Client: Well, most people have more interesting things to say than I have, and I feel inferior. I know that I put myself down, and this is a big problem. I don't know how to handle it; I just don't know.

Counselor: It sounds like you've gotten into a habit of counting yourself out, and perhaps it offers some benefits to your well-being. You don't have to take risks; it's safer and more comfortable to stay within old patterns. It takes some energy and effort to break out of those patterns.

Client: I know I just tend to sit back. Quite often I feel like I'm invisible in a group, and that makes it even worse. Then I feel like there is nothing that I can do but sit back and listen.

Counselor: Well, it seems like you are saying that others are excluding you, whereas in reality perhaps you are excluding yourself. You feel excluded, but others are not deliberately excluding you. You are the one holding back.

Client: Yes, but that comes from the fear of appearing stupid. How does one overcome that? It just seems to be happening all the time.

Counselor: You are saying that it's easier to sit back than it is to take the risk and appear stupid. I'm saying that sometimes if you want to be included you have to take that risk; you have to actively make a place for yourself; you have to poke in there.

Client: That is pretty difficult for me to do.

Counselor: I know it's tough; I believe that. But if you want to be included, it will be necessary for you to assert yourself. You see, things stay the same unless we make some effort to change them. That's the hard part.

Client: That is hard.

Counselor: I know it's hard. Why don't we practice, here.

Transcript of Role Play #2

Client: When I was younger I felt like I could handle anything. Since being home with the kids, I'm not sure what I could do.

Counselor: Well, it sounds like you've done a good job at home with the kids. I'll bet that some of those skills and abilities that you've developed at home could be used to do other things as well.

Client: Everything I do is so routine. I feel like I've become a real boring person.

Counselor: Well, that is certainly a tough way to feel, but I can understand how you might feel that way doing the same things every day and not feeling that anything is a challenge to you anymore.

Client: Especially doing housework! It gets me totally depressed, and no one appreciates it at all.

Counselor: Housework certainly can be routine, and as a maintenance job it is one that doesn't get noticed unless it's left undone. If it doesn't offer you any satisfaction, why not consider spending your time doing something that is more likely to provide you with satisfaction?

Client: I have thought about doing other things, but my children always come first with me. I think it's important that a mother be there for her children when they come home from school, don't you?

Counselor: It's probably important that children have some supervision, but that doesn't necessarily have to be provided by you. Your needs are important, too. If you are not happy, it's likely that the children will be aware of that.

Client: I don't know why I'm unhappy. My kids are good; my husband is caring.

Counselor: Well, you've always been an active, involved person. Your kids needed you more when they were younger; now you have more time for yourself. This is a great chance for you to start thinking about all those things you've wanted to do but didn't have a chance to earlier.

Client: I think it might be kind of late for me to start thinking about a different career.

Counselor: Not at all! You haven't just been vegetating at home; you've been developing as a person, maturing, using all kinds of skills in organizing, managing, and so on. You might need some further training to sharpen up those skills, but I think you have a lot to offer. You certainly have the capability. You've experienced the dissatisfaction of not using your abilities. This is a good time to plan some moves.

Client: I feel like I've been vegetating, but perhaps you're right. But I just don't feel very confident.

Counselor: No, I'm sure you don't. That happens to a lot of women who stay at home. But it won't take long, once you start doing something, for that confidence to return. Confidence is simply the result of practice with positive feedback. You just have to start doing things, and you'll find the confidence returning.

Client: I wish I felt as positive as you do.

Counselor: I'm positive because I've seen it happen to others, and I'm sure the same will be true for you.

Transcript of Role Play #3

Client: Since I've been on my own, I feel like my children neglect me and my friends don't come around very often. I feel totally abandoned!

Counselor: Sometimes children and friends don't seem very helpful because they really don't know what to do. Perhaps you've reached a point where there is little others can do for you, and you have to do things for yourself.

Client: Sometimes I feel like my children are ashamed of me sitting here alone, doing nothing. They keep telling me to find something to do, to keep busy.

Counselor: I can understand that it's rather difficult to hear that from your children. After all, for the last twenty years or so you've been very busy just looking after them. But that doesn't mean that they are likely to spend the next twenty years looking after you.

Client: Well, I don't expect that! I do expect some consideration, though, some effort on their part.

Counselor: You know, they have probably always thought of you as the person with the answers, the person who could solve problems, the person who could cope. Maybe they don't even see you as a person in need.

Client: I always taught them to be considerate of others, and now they don't even spare a thought to their own mother.

Counselor: I think we've established that for whatever reason your children are not going to get you out of your current gloom. Let's try to think of some ways that you can do things to get you out and moving.

Client: I don't know where to begin, where to even start.

Counselor: Well, a good place to start is in your own neighborhood. There is a community center close by; there is a church not too far away; there is a park down the street where you could go for walks.

Client: Well, I've never been much of a joiner, and I don't really enjoy walking.

Counselor: I guess some of those things don't sound too appealing if you've never done them before. But I would venture that they are worth a try. Trying new things can be a bit uncomfortable at first, but if you get over that initial discomfort, you may find that they're quite enjoyable.

Client: I'd feel a lot better about doing things if I had somebody else to do them with.

Counselor: A lot of women feel that way because they are less accustomed to being independent. You may be able to find someone to do things with, but you will probably also have to become accustomed to doing things by yourself. That can be enjoyable, too.

Client: I'll check with my daughter about some of the things at the community center.

Counselor: That's a good place to start, but don't be disappointed if she isn't able to go with you. It doesn't mean that she doesn't care, just that she is busy. . . . And that might be your big chance to do something on your own.

Client: That would sure surprise everybody.

Counselor: And what a nice surprise it would be!

MEASUREMENT OF ENCOURAGEMENT OF TOTAL DEVELOPMENT

Role-playing exercises can also be evaluated more formally using the Encouragement of Total Development Scale that is given below. Increasing levels of the scale indicate increased depth and breadth of the counselor's encouragement of both self-attending and androgynous behaviors in clients. The scale was originally developed to measure ten counselor responses to a script of ten different client statements (Russell, 1982). The numerical values refer to total specified responses during counseling exchanges of that duration.

The scale thus measures the extent to which counselors encourage their clients to explore, develop, or enhance activities that focus on themselves and stress mastery, self-fulfillment, and total self-development. These activities may be perceived to be in opposition to or in conflict with traditional female, other-centered activities. In brief, this scale measures the extent to which counselors give clients encouragement to consider self-nurturing, self-developing behaviors as primary and foremost.

At the lowest scale level, counselors do not provide any encouragement, provide encouragement without indicating a preferred direction for development, or encourage stereotypically feminine development only. The second level responses include encouragement of self-development only as a secondary function. The third level of skill performance includes clear and direct encouragement of total development coupled with the recognition that conflict with traditional behaviors and expectations may ensue. At the fourth level, there is strong encouragement to pursue androgynous goals. Finally, at the fifth level, the integration of male and female traits is stressed as ideal and maximally beneficial to individual flexibility and effectiveness.

ENCOURAGEMENT OF TOTAL DEVELOPMENT SCALE

Level I

The counselor either provides no encouragement whatsoever, provides diffuse, directionless encouragement, or only encourages traditional, other-directed activities.

Key Words: *Nondirectional or other-directional*

Level II

The counselor encourages self-development only as additional to or an extension of traditional, other-directed activities. Minimal disruption to traditional female role functions is encouraged.

Key Words: *Self-development secondary*

Level III

The counselor makes at least one response that stresses development that is primarily self-focused and that may be in conflict with traditional female role expectations. The counselor indicates that gender is not a valid basis for restricting behavior.

Key Words: *Beginning encouragement of self-development*

Level IV

The counselor encourages self-attending in at least two statements. Androgynous development is described as desirable, and self-neglect is linked to personal distress and dysfunction.

Key Words: *Emphasize desirability of total development*

Level V

The counselor emphasizes the benefits of integration of male and female traits in increasing personal competence, mastery, and self-fulfillment. Total development is described as the primary counseling goal.

Key Words: *Total development primary*

CLINICAL APPLICATIONS

Women seeking counseling frequently perceive themselves as inadequate and unable to cope with the multifaceted demands made upon them. Alternately, women seek counseling because of a basic dissatisfaction with their current life situation and predominating activities. The skill of encouraging total development can be used by a counselor to assist her clients to reevaluate their current situation for both strengths and weaknesses and to plan realistic ways of acquiring any requisite behaviors or capabilities that will lead to greater satisfaction.

Using the skill of encouraging total development, the counselor can aid the client first in attending to herself, in examining her own needs, wants, and desires, and second in developing the neglected aspects of her total being with the goal of becoming a truly androgynous person. Androgynous development is a clearly stated goal of feminist counseling, as it maximizes personal flexibility and ability to cope with the variety of situations to be found in the modern world.

The counselor's encouragement of total development may need to be continuous and sustained, as women have been socialized to be primarily other directed and feminine. The goals of attending to the self and developing androgynous capacities, therefore, may seem both foreign and initially unacceptable to some women. Attending to the self may be construed as selfish, neglectful of significant others, or egocentric. Guilt, remorse, and shame may accompany initial endeavors in this regard. Counselor encouragement, therefore, needs to be accompanied by explanations of the source of these negative reactions. A counselor can counter negative personal reactions as well as negative social reactions with a feminist analysis demonstrating the validity of total development goals.

Encouragement of androgynous development, likewise, may be beset with both initial negative personal reactions by the client and negative feedback from her social network. The client will possibly feel deprived of the benefits of traditionally feminine traits; traits such as dependence and passivity may have served her after a fashion in the past. A counselor must be able to offer encouragement for the development of traits that may be perceived as conflicting with feminine traits, to provide a perspective that legitimizes such development, and to explain how situational determinants rather than gender limitations are most effective in governing behavior.

Androgynous development is likely also to elicit negative social reactions both at the interpersonal level, where androgynous development may necessitate a reallocation of power within relationships, and at the larger social level, where the exclusive domination by males may be threatened by women's demands. A counselor using the skill of encouraging total development, therefore, will need not only to encourage but also to alert or warn her clients about these possible negative repercussions. The emphasis, clearly, remains on the benefits to clients and ultimately to women generally.

As has been indicated throughout this chapter, the skill of encouraging total development may frequently be used in conjunction with the skill of social analysis. The social analysis provides the perspective or the rationale, while the encouragement of total development indicates the direction or provides the specific goals for the client to pursue. Total development as a goal may initially seem quite unacceptable to many women clients unless they are first provided with the social analysis, which places it into a social perspective.

Encouragement of total development may also need to be supplemented with the skill of positive evaluation of women. Many women feel that they are personally inadequate or incapable of pursuing androgynous development. Female socialization has instilled a sense of personal limitation. Counselors may need to dispel this myth of female inadequacy before clients can actively pursue total development of the self.

In using the skill of encouraging total development, many counselors may find that a client is unaware of many of her behaviors and traits that the counselor is suggesting as targets of change. Female socialization is not only pervasive but can also be insidious and subtle, below the conscious awareness of the individual.

A client's social consciousness may have been raised by the counselor's social analysis, but her awareness of the impact of female socialization on her own behavior and attitudes may not have been similarly heightened. The skill of encouraging total development, therefore, may also have to be used in conjunction with another skill designed for this purpose, the skill of behavior feedback.

Encouraging total self-development is best facilitated when a client is clearly aware that her tendencies have been to focus on others and to rely on stereotypic female behavior in the past. To provide clients with such awareness, the counselor may need to develop the skill of behavior feedback. This counseling skill is the focus of the next chapter.

Chapter 7

THE SKILL OF BEHAVIOR FEEDBACK

THE SKILL DEFINED

Behavior feedback is the counseling skill of providing clients with accurate and concise feedback regarding their behavior or behavioral manifestations of affect. Effective feedback includes reports of observed discrepancies between client statements and counselor observations, between client statements and client behavior, and between client self-perceptions and perceptions of ideal self. In this regard, behavior feedback resembles the technique of confrontation that is an acknowledged component of many counseling approaches (e.g. Carkhuff, 1969). However, behavior feedback in feminist counseling differs from confrontation of more traditional feedback techniques in both form and intent.

The intent of behavior feedback in feminist counseling is to provide the client with concrete, specific information that she can evaluate for herself in terms of its accuracy and relevance. The client is encouraged to respond to the feedback, to discuss it with the counselor, to engage in a dialogue between equals regarding its veracity and its significance to the current situation.

This intent is contrary to that of traditional approaches, in which the counselor's feedback is frequently enmeshed in psychodynamic interpretations, psychiatric diagnoses, or intrapsychic prescriptions. By providing this kind of feedback the counselor places herself clearly in the position of expert with the client having little option in response. The counselor in effect makes the statement that she knows more about the client than the client knows about herself and that she will brook no argument in this regard. An authoritarian, didactic position is therefore presented and upheld.

Behavior feedback in feminist counseling aims to foster an

egalitarian client-counselor relationship in two ways. First, by emphasizing the concrete and observable aspects of the client's behavior, the counselor is dealing with events that are equally evident to herself and the client. The counselor is not mystifying or making more complex what is observed; she is simply reporting what she sees. The client can therefore respond on the same level. The client can agree with the counselor's perception, she can reserve judgement, or she can disagree. Behavior feedback encourages this kind of dialogue by asking the client for her response.

Secondly, by using behavior feedback in the concrete, specific, feminist sense, the counselor is modeling a monitoring process that the client can readily understand and learn. The counselor is demonstrating that by observing or noting one's behaviors and/or affect and by paying particular attention to discrepancies, one can learn a great deal about one's psychological functioning. Through this demonstration the counselor can provide the client with instruction on how to monitor her own behavior in the future. The counselor thereby indicates to the client that the techniques used in counseling are not mysterious or enigmatic but understandable skills that the client can learn and apply herself. The inequality between counselor and client is thus minimized, and clients can obtain skills that will enable them to deal with problems more independently in the future.

Striving for an equal client-counselor relationship by demystifying the counseling process and by transferring counseling skills to the client is a central tenet of feminist counseling. Initially, the relationship between counselors and clients is clearly not one between equals, as the client is in the position of depending on the counselor for help. An egalitarian stance at this early point in the encounter is likely to be dysfunctional. Clients need to trust counselors as sources of strength when they themselves feel lacking in strength. Clients endow counselors with *expert power*, the power to provide help based on their superior knowledge and expertise. Counselors, in accepting to help clients, acknowledge this expert power. In feminist counseling, however, counselors must then proceed to disperse this knowledge to clients, using behavior feedback and other feminist counseling skills.

The skill of behavior feedback is, therefore, used by feminist counselors to provide clients with two different types of information. First, clients are provided with information about their own behavior, which can be a focus for counseling. Second, clients are provided with information about how to deal with their difficulties more effectively in the future. Clients thereby receive not only remedial current help but also tools for applying remedies independently or avoiding problems altogether in the future. Feminist counselors are not jealous or protective of their expertise. Rather, they are intent on sharing knowledge so that women generally can be more more effective and powerful in the future.

The form as well as the intent of behavior feedback is distinctive in feminist counseling. The form of feedback is similar to behavioral approaches to counseling, as the name suggests. Feminist counselors do not deny the importance of internal processes as some behaviorists do, but they do avoid diagnosing and labeling these processes. Instead, feminist counselors phrase their feedback in terms of that which is observable and can be readily monitored by client and counselor alike. Feminist counselors refrain, for example, from telling a client that she looks depressed, instead commenting on her lethargy, downcast expression, or lack of demonstrable affect. A client then has the opportunity to provide an interpretation of these observations. Perhaps the client herself will state that indeed she is feeling depressed, but alternately she may state that these behaviors reflect the result of a strenuous social engagement the night before.

Behavior feedback, therefore, reports to the client, accurately and concisely, the observations of the client by the counselor. The observations are concrete in that they relate to the specific behaviors of the client or the behavioral manifestations of affect. The observations may relate to fairly minute behavioral manifestations, such as drumming fingers, a slight frown, a hesitation in speech, and so on. The interpretation of these behaviors, however, is left to the client. Counselors may ask clients about perceived meanings of the behaviors. Counselors may suggest that these behaviors sometimes indicate affective states such as anxiety, uncertainty, ambivalence, etc., but final interpretations are left to the client.

Behavior feedback, with its emphasis on presenting behaviors, results in a counseling technique that has a distinctive here-and-now focus. Feminist counselors do not deny the impact of preadult developmental history, but they are principally concerned with current situations, current problems, and current solutions. Using the skill of behavior feedback, feminist counselors aim to influence the present behavior of clients directly rather than through hypothetical constructs, such as unconscious motivation or other intrapsychic mechanisms. Behavior feedback directly addresses those behaviors which are in need of remedy.

Some clients may enter counseling with the expectation that understanding of personal dynamics or insight into psychological processes will automatically result in problem resolution. These clients may expect to focus on their past in counseling. It may be necessary for a counselor to explain to her client that although prior psychological development has served to establish patterns and acquire behaviors, current behaviors are what needs to be changed, and such change can only occur in the present.

Because of the focus on the present in feminist counseling, the interaction between client and counselor, too, can become a counseling focus. The counselor not only feeds back her observations about the client but can also indicate how the client's behavior affects her. The relationship between client and counselor can be regarded as the prototype of client realtionships. Many of the coping strategies and behavioral patterns that the clients use in daily interactions are likely to occur some time in the counseling session. Clients can benefit from receiving feedback about the reactions their behavior engenders in others.

Role playing can be used to amplify the effectiveness of behavior feedback in counseling. Behavioral rehearsal can help clients to acquire new behaviors, which can be shaped by behavior feedback from the counselor. Some clients may initially find rehearsal or role playing somewhat artificial, but counselors can emphasize the benefits of practice in preparing for a particular encounter. Counselors can also alleviate initial anxiety by themselves participating actively in the role playing, beginning by acting out the role of the client, asking the client for feedback, and then encouraging the client to demonstrate the way that it "should be done." Both client and counselor behaviors then become the subject and focus of the clinical process, particularly as they relate to the problems at hand.

FEEDBACK OF DISCREPANCIES

Behavior feedback is most effective when it relates to observed discrepancies. Discrepancies can occur in many different spheres, and discrepancies can frequently be observed between the client's real self and the client's ideal self. Women frequently experience this, since the notion of an ideal woman is generally unrealistic, unattainable, and constantly changing.

The traditionally idealized woman was required to be totally devoted to home and family, supplying unending compassion, understanding, succor, and support for her family. This ideal woman was supposed to be totally and completely competent in managing a home, directing the activities of her children, and planning and organizing the social life for the family; yet, she needed her husband or a "more capable" male to handle matters that were not home related. These paradoxical requirements of meeting her own needs only through fulfilling the needs of others and of being totally competent in one sphere while totally dependent in another were ones that women strove to incorporate into their own lives in attempting to meet their ideal. It is not surprising that so many women fell short of reaching an ideal that was ultimately unattainable.

The ideal modern woman represents a goal that is no more attainable. This idealized figure combines total commitment to a career with total commitment to her family and complete responsibility for household management. This is all accomplished without a hair out of place, without a bead of perspiration on her brow, without a crease in her designer dress, and without raising her voice. This super-woman can accomplish anything she sets out to do without any visible stress, appearing serious yet attractive all the while. This ideal woman puts to shame all the women who are "only" homemakers, all those who run themselves ragged managing a home and outside job, and all those who find that the requirements of a job necessitate large amounts of assistance in the home. This ideal, no less than that of the traditional woman, is unattainable and by its nature fosters feelings of inadequacy in women.

Coupled with these socially prescribed notions of the ideal women, each woman usually has her own notions of what an ideal woman should be like. These notions are frequently derived from her observations of her own mother or of other adult women that she observed in her formative years. Sometimes the ideal is to emulate these women; at other times the ideal is to be unlike these other women. In either case, it is likely that concepts of the ideal reflect a partial and superficial understanding of the idealized women, which makes it unlikely that attainment of the ideal will be reached.

Behavior feedback can be used to aid clients in reexamining their notions of the ideal self, particularly as they relate to unattainable models. The client's feelings of inadequacy are likely to persist until she can learn to reject the unattainable components of such ideals and realign her ideals to accord with reality. Behavior feedback from the counselor can aid in this process by presenting the discrepancies to the client in a nonjudgmental, constructive fashion.

Another frequently encountered discrepancy is that between the client's perception of herself and the counselor's perception of her. Many clients presenting themselves for counseling have totally succumbed to social notions of women, including themselves, as helpless, incapable, and incompetent. They have been overwhelmed by social evaluations of themselves as having second-class status as women. They may have been involved in relationships wherein they were subjected to a continual barrage of messages describing them as incompetent, failures in their roles and aspirations, and not worthy of love or respect.

Yet, in spite of these negative messages, many of these women have managed to care for themselves and their families. This then, could be identified in the course of behavior feedback as a major achievement and capitalized as a component of self-perception. Many clients dismiss their positive accomplishments because they see the accomplishments as basic and necessary tasks rather than extraordinary attainments in the face of considerable adversity. Many women are not able to appraise themselves and their strengths realistically because they have so thoroughly internalized all the impossible "shoulds" and "oughts" of womanhood. A counselor using behavior feedback can begin to demonstrate that indeed these accomplishments represent considerable personal strength and fortitude and belie the notion of the helpless, incompetent woman.

Sometimes the feedback regarding the discrepancy between the counselor's perception of the woman and her self-perception can have a more negative tone. Women frequently complain of not being taken seriously, not being listened to, not being offered the extent of respect they feel is their due. Sometimes, however, their ineffectiveness relates to the manner in which they make requests or demands. Women have been socialized to speak in a low and gentle voice, to avert their eyes, to smile while speaking, and to suppress their anger. All of these behaviors detract from the seriousness and urgency of their message. A "little girl" approach may periodically be effective in securing certain favors from a loved one but is unlikely to be effective in most interpersonal transactions. Many women are unaware how their demeanor and self-presentation can detract from their effectiveness. A counselor using behavior feedback can demonstrate to the client that her behavior contradicts her message, that the way in which she delivers the message detracts from its effect, and that female socialization needs to be overcome to increase effectiveness.

Behavior feedback can also be used to relate observed discrepancies between a client's actions and her statements. Many women continually voice dissatisfaction with innumerable aspects of their lives but take no action to improve them. Dissatisfaction is frequently voiced about relationships; anger is expressed at being taken for granted; rage is expressed at perceived abuse. These reports, however, are presented to a third party such as a friend or relative rather than to the person who is the perceived cause. Women's sense of powerlessness and fear of abandonment explain this lack of direct action, but counselors can use behavior feedback to demonstrate that such ventilation alone is unlikely to result in any change in the situation. As clients become aware of this discrepancy and its futility, they can consciously decide how to resolve it—whether by living with the situation and accepting it or by taking some confrontative action to change it. Counselors can couple this behavior feedback with feedback about the client's strengths to increase feelings of competence in regard to potential actions. However, the choice regarding the manner in which the discrepancy will be handled remains with the client.

Behavior feedback as used by the feminist counselor can, therefore, yield clients useful information not only about their current behavior but also about the discrepancies or conflicts found in it. These discrepancies between the ideal self and the perceived self, between self-perception and the counselor's perception of the client, between statements and actions, can be presented by the counselor to motivate clients, to aid in their self-affirmation, to increase their positive self-perception, and to provide material for behavior change. The feedback is objective because counselors report what they perceive; they do not label or diagnose. Counselors may follow up observations with questions regarding possible motives or explanations for the observed behavior, but the final interpretation about those motives is left to the client. Thus, the process becomes very much a shared process that contrasts with the pronouncements of more traditional counseling practices.

LEVELS OF BEHAVIOR FEEDBACK

The skill of behavior feedback can be used at several different levels depending upon the particular phase of the counseling process and the counselor's commitment and ability to use the skill. The use of this skill is less dependent upon client characteristics in that behavior feedback is so basic that it makes minimal demands on a client's comprehension ability and/or cognitive skills. Indeed, the only requirement is that the client be ready to accept feedback.

The levels of behavior feedback skill are set by the orientation, philosophy, and clinical style of the counselor. At the lowest level of the behavior feedback skill, counselors do not respond to the specific behavior of the client. Instead, they make general statements that frequently include psychodynamic references and/or interpretations or diagnoses of clients. At this level, counselors use their expertise and understanding of client psychological processes to distance themselves from clients, rather than developing an egalitarian process.

Counselors at the second level of behavior feedback offer general responses that are relatively verifiable and thus offer the potential for a two-way process. The lack of concreteness and specificity, however, detracts from this goal. The counselor is demonstrating a commitment to an egalitarian process but is less skilled at it than she could be.

At the third level, counselors offer a clear and concise feedback that includes references to discrepancies. At the fourth level, not only are discrepancies reported, but client strengths are maximized to increase the clients' feelings of competence to deal with the discrepancies.

At the highest level of the behavior feedback skill, counselors not only feed back discrepancies with emphasis on the positive aspects of behavior but also request client affirmation or disputation of the observations. At the highest level, therefore, counselors not only provide feedback that is verifiable but also ensure that this process of verification takes place. In doing so, counselors accept the possibility of receiving negative feedback from clients, much the same as clients can receive negative feedback from counselors. Counselors thus endow their clients with power that approximates their own in the counseling relationship.

In judging the appropriate level of behavior feedback to be used, counselors need to consider primarily the rate and timing of feedback in relation to the phase of the counseling process. Most clients can accept behavior feedback at a surface level from the beginning of the counseling encounter. Increases in the intensity and depth of feedback follow in relation to the ability of the client to assimilate feedback. It is not likely, for example, that a counselor would begin pointing out discrepancies to a client in the initial counseling encounter. The counselor would want to ensure that a counseling relationship was firmly established before making such observations. Likewise, a counselor might begin by feeding back positive observations but might wait until a later phase of the counseling process to feed back those observations which might be construed as negative. The client's readiness to use the behavior feedback is therefore a primary consideration in the level and type of feedback presented.

REQUIREMENTS FOR SKILL ACQUISITION

To acquire the skill of behavior feedback, the counselor must have an awareness of its relevance, a commitment to its function, and an ability to communicate it unambiguously.

Awareness

Counselors intending to use behavior feedback need to develop an awareness of relevant client behavior to attend to and report, as well as indications of discrepancies apparent in client functioning. Counselors also need to develop an awareness of their own reactions to client behaviors because these reactions indicate the effects of such behaviors. For example, clients may behave in ways that produce defensive counselor reactions. Counselors who are aware of their own defensiveness can then feed back to clients their reactions and examine both the motivation and intent of the client as well as their own response.

This awareness of client and self is basic to counseling, and feminist counseling differs only slightly in the focus and emphasis of the awareness. Feminist counselors are particularly mindful of those behaviors and reactions that are reinforced by female sex role socialization. Passive, dependent, self-denying behaviors, therefore, frequently become the subject of counselor feedback in feminist counseling.

Conviction

The counselor commitment to behavior feedback results basically from her endorsement of the feminist philosophy and rejection of the all-encompassing intrapsychic focus. Additionally, the counselor's commitment to this counseling skill rests on the acceptance of the primacy of self-development and the benefits of androgynous development. Counselors may need to free themselves of vestiges of stereotypic thinking in order to endorse fully these counseling goals. Social reinforcements for feminine self-denial and feminine behavior are still powerful, and counselors and clients alike may need support in pursuing goals not recognized by society. Like their clients, counselors, too, can benefit from the support of peer groups in maintaining their commitment to this and other aspects of the feminist counseling approach.

Communication

Communication of behavior feedback, while seemingly uncomplicated, can in fact present several difficulties for feminist counselors. These difficulties reflect in part the conceptual shifts that are required in moving from abstract skills, such as social analysis, to concrete skills, such as behavior feedback. Also, they reflect the shift from the jargon-laden language of counseling education and literature to the simple, straightforward communication required in counseling. Lastly, counselors may experience difficulties in relinquishing the authority and expertise inherent in complex psychological terminology and relying instead on the basic terms of behavior feedback.

Maximally effective communication of behavior feedback is simple, direct, concrete, and open to verification or disputation. It lacks complexity, abstractness, and professional jargon. Counselors must translate their own awareness of significant observations, which may be complex and abstract, into simple, concrete terms. This requires absolute clarity in the counselor's thinking as well as skill in making the translation. It does no good to hide fuzzy thinking behind abstract terminology when simple, direct statements are required.

This difficulty in presenting concrete statements is further compounded by the interrelationship of behavior feedback with several other feminist counseling skills that are by nature abstract and theoretical. Feminist counselors frequently preface behavior feedback with social analysis or positive evaluation of women. Both these skills can be highly abstract; hence, counselors must be skilled not only in making transitions between skills but also in making transitions in their levels of abstractness.

Avoiding complex and jargon-laden counseling language also communicates a commitment to a more egalitarian client-counselor relationship. Complex or obscure jargon can create an illusion of counselor competency regardless of the actual level of counselor skill. Simple, direct, and concrete language, on the other hand, mitigates against such illusions, and counseling skill is only manifest in counseling effects rather than in the language that is used. Discarding the use of complex language and clinical jargon is, therefore, analogous to the stripping of authoritative trappings. Doing so, the counselor comes to rely upon the bare bones of clinical understanding and counseling skill. Inasmuch as this involves a voluntary surrender of power by the counselor, it needs to rest firmly on a commitment to and conviction about the benefits of egalitarianism in counseling.

Counselors with awareness and commitment should not find it difficult to master the skill of communicating observations in specific, concrete, observable terms. Counselors can benefit from requesting clients to provide feedback regarding the ease of understanding and relevance of counselor communication as they perceive it. Clients can thus provide behavior feedback to aid counselors, just as counselors provide feedback for clients. Counselors who check out the veracity and specificity of their behavior feedback with clients are exercising both the spirit and the intent of the behavior feedback skill.

THE SUPPORTING RESEARCH

Behavior feedback has not been empirically investigated as a discrete counseling skill. However, there are several sources of indirect evidence that bears on an evaluation of the effectiveness of behavior feedback in counseling. Behavior feedback is an element of many of the behavioral approaches to counseling, which have had considerable success in shaping and molding behavior.

Kazdin (1978) notes in his review of operant techniques with clinical populations that behavior feedback is a component of many behavior change packages. The learning of social skills by delinquent girls, the development and maintenance of self-care tasks in prison populations, and the acquisition of skills by behavior-change agents are all examples of behaviors that have been successfully increased by behavior feedback. Rosenthal and Bandura (1978) likewise note that behavior feedback is frequently coupled with modeling to produce significant increases in verbal expressiveness, assertive behavior, and social competence. While behavior feedback is not always the most powerful aspect of these behavior change packages, it nevertheless makes a contribution to the behavior change of the client. It can therefore be argued that behavior feedback is likely to have a similar impact in the context of feminist counseling skills as it does in the context of other behaviorally oriented counseling techniques.

While there is a lack of direct empirical evidence for the skill of behavior feedback, experience in related areas strongly suggests that it significantly affects the reality of counseling. Behaviorally, this skill provides the client with information and/or data on which she can choose to act or not act. Information is a source of power, and that applies no less to the individual or personal level than to the social or political level.

The political consequences of behavior feedback include reinforcement of feelings of strength and power in individual women in relationships, which they can later transfer into the public arena. The counselor in promoting equality in counseling anticipates the equal participation of women in society.

CLINICAL EXAMPLES

The following case description represents a synopsis of an actual clinical case that was presented to a number of experienced feminist counselors. Each of the counselors responded to the client presentation in her own clinical style. The variety of responses is presented here to demonstrate how the skill of behavior feedback can be modified and diversified depending on individual inclinations. Each counseling response will be followed by an analytical comment discussing the probable intent and meaning of the counseling response.

The Case of Audrey Jones

Audrey was a twenty-six-year-old married woman living with her husband and eight-month-old infant in a university family residence. Audrey was an only child of a professional family and had high expectations for a professional career prior to her marriage. Upon marriage Audrey opted to leave school to support her husband's postgraduate studies, much to the dismay of her family. The pregnancy that followed shortly thereafter was perceived as untimely by all concerned. Audrey sought counseling because of feelings of constant fatigue, doubts about her effectiveness as a mother, and despair at her husband's lack of caring and emotional support.

Audrey: I think I must be neurotic or something. Here I have a lovely baby and a good husband, and I just feel rotten. My husband's work is very important, and I'm not helping him the way I should because I'm so tired and on edge. I can't make my husband understand the way I feel, and I'm probably not being too clear to you, either.

Counselor A: Audrey, you are being perfectly clear and making very good sense. You're not neurotic because you feel dissatisfied with your situation. Your situation is one of high demand and high stress, and coupled with your high expectations of yourself it is very likely to lead to fatigue, anxiety, and even feelings of depression. You have been very capable in the past, but now you are faced with a whole new set of expectations, new skills to master, and new responsibilities to take on. I think it might help to look at what you are expecting of yourself. Shall we do that?

Comment: Counselor A is using behavior feedback to focus on the positive traits that Audrey has exhibited in the past and is exhibiting in the present. Frequently clients become overwhelmed with their perceived inadequacies and lose sight of what they have accomplished and what is reasonable for them to accomplish now. Counselor A is suggesting that Audrey has a discrepancy between her ideal self and perceived self and is indicating that this discrepancy might be a fruitful avenue to explore further.

Counselor B: You know, Audrey, I find it hard to believe that you and I are talking about the same person. You describe her as neurotic, incompetent, and incomprehensible, and I see before me a person who is articulate, well spoken, and dealing very competently with her baby (who is obviously thriving) and seems to be very much in charge of her life. I've also heard a lot of frustration expressed about being a wife and mother and no longer a student pursuing your own goals. I wonder if that frustration is getting in the way of seeing yourself clearly. What do you think about that?

Comment: Counselor B is focusing on the discrepancy between Audrey's perception of herself and the image she presents to others. The counselor is speculating on the reasons for this discrepancy and relating this to Audrey's earlier statements about her situation as a homemaker. The counselor is presenting this as a suggestion to Audrey and asking for her opinion. Although the feedback in the latter part of the statement is not strictly behavioral, it is offered in such a way as to encourage refutation or agreement.

Counselor C: Audrey, what you've been saying to me is that you want to be more of a help to your husband, although it's not clear how you could accomplish that or whether he wants or needs it. You've also been saying that you want to be more of a help to your baby, although, again, he seems to be doing just fine. I wonder if what your body might be saying, by being always tired, and what your mind might be saying, by feeling stressed, is that you really need more help, more support, more understanding with the very important job that you are doing. What do you think of that? Do you think that might apply to you?

Comment: Counselor C is feeding back to Audrey the discrepancy that she perceives between what Audrey is verbalizing and what her nonverbal messages seem to be. The nonverbal messages could be interpreted as requests for help even while Audrey's verbal assertion is that she must help others more than she is doing. The counselor does not, however, simply present this as an interpretation. She feeds back what she perceives as a discrepancy and asks Audrey for her confirmation or disagreement. In addition, the counselor is feeding back the positives regarding Audrey's functioning in her present role.

These three examples provide some indication of the way in which counselors can utilize behavior feedback to reinforce the perceived strengths of the client, to point out discrepancies between the counselor's perceptions and the client's perceptions and/or actions, and to ask the client for validation or disputation of the behavioral observations. In each case, the counselor is responding to what she perceives to be the most salient aspect of the client's statement. The counselor responds in a way that she believes will be most helpful to the client. The counselor makes an assessment of what she believes the client needs to hear and structures her feedback accordingly.

In each of these instances, the counselor is attempting to keep her language at a simple and concrete level so that her observations may be validated by the client. Instead of speaking of unconscious mechanisms, for example, Counselor C reports observations of body language and suggests a particular meaning. She recognizes, however, that the body language may represent something else entirely, and the client is given an opportunity to provide an alternate explanation.

Behavior feedback, therefore, can serve as a dynamic facilitator of the counseling process in encouraging the exchange between counselor and client. It may initially appear simple or even simpleminded when compared to complex intrapsychic interpretations and diagnoses, but evidence suggests that results may be equally if not more positive.

The role-playing exercises given here allow for experimentation with this counseling skill. Participants are encouraged to try different and varied responses with the view to moving from the simple or lower levels of the skill to the higher skill levels. With behavior feedback, as with any other counseling skill, practice and experimentation will reveal the potential use and effectiveness of the skill in clinical practice.

ROLE-PLAYING EXERCISES

Role Play #1

Client: I feel so ignorant. I feel like I don't have anything interesting to say in a conversation.
Counselor:

Role Play #2

Client: I know that I have a very low opinion of myself. I don't have much confidence in my ability to do anything. Is that be-

cause of my childhood, the way may parents treated me?
Counselor:

Role Play #3

Client: I'm old and worn out. I'm no longer attractive or good to anybody. I'm not needed by anybody, and most people just regard me as a nuisance.
Counselor:

As with role playing in the counseling techniques described earlier, this has the following requirements:

1. Two participants alternating roles
2. Recording role plays on audio- or videotapes
3. Review and critique of each role play
4. Review of the corresponding transcript of the feminist counselor's response
5. Discussion of possible modifications of role plays in view of considered responses in transcripts
6. Role reenactment with modifications

In the process of examining the initial role playing of the behavior feedback skill, the participants may wish to include the following considerations:

1. Was the language simple, concrete, and related to observable events?
2. Was the language at a level that could easily be understood by the client, that is, was it jargon-free?
3. Did the feedback include positive client attributes?
4. Did the feedback include perceived discrepancies?
5. Was the client encouraged to verify and/or refute the counselor's perceptions?
6. Was the feedback likely to maximize or diminish the client's sense of personal power?
7. To what extent did the feedback foster an egalitarian client-counselor relationship?

The above questions are suggestions or guidelines for analyzing the role playing. Suggestions for alternative or modified responses may also be found in the transcripts of role enactments that follow.

ROLE-PLAYING TRANSCRIPTS

The following transcripts are examples of how experienced feminist counselors responded to the client statements in the role plays presented earlier in this chapter. It bears repeating that these transcripts are offered as examples, not prescriptions, of the behavior feedback skill. Just as each of the counselors in the following transcripts used behavior feedback in her own way, so may any novice skill user want to integrate behavior feedback into her own style. The transcripts can provide the novice with ideas, suggestions, and indications of how this integration may be achieved.

Transcript of Role Play #1

Client: I feel so ignorant. I feel like I don't have anything interesting to say in a conversation.

Counselor: You've told me a lot of interesting things about yourself. Don't you think that others might also be interested in hearing about them?

Client: Well, I don't like to talk about myself. People who do talk about themselves all the time are so . . . so self-centered.

Counselor: That may be so, but it's difficult to have a conversation without putting a little of yourself into it. You have to make some aspect of yourself known, whether it be your opinions, or thoughts, or whatever, so that others can respond to it.

Client: I guess so, but I'd rather find out about what others are thinking.

Counselor: And how would you go about doing that?

Client: I guess by asking questions.

Counselor: That's terrific! You know, I find that most people are more than happy to talk about themselves. Asking questions is one of the best ways to get involved in a conversation.

Client: The only problem with that is that I'm afraid that my questions will sound stupid or ignorant.

Counselor: I haven't found that any questions that you've asked me have been stupid or ignorant. You ask very good and perceptive questions. I can't believe that the questions that you ask other people would be completely different.

Client: But I feel that I know you. I don't have to pretend with you.

Counselor: And how do you have to pretend with others?

Client: I have to pretend that I'm more interesting and exciting than I really am.

Counselor: Hmmm, so is it true that you are a dull, boring person who never has anything interesting to say, never has done an exciting or interesting thing in her whole life, never has thought an interesting or profound thought in all her days?

Client: (laughs)

Counselor: Well, is it? Is what I just said true?

Client: No, of course not.

Counselor: So what I said earlier about you is more true—that I find you interesting, and so would other people.

Client: I guess that might be so.

Transcript of Role Play #2

Client: I know that I have a very low opinion of myself. I don't have much confidence in my ability to do anything. Is that because of my childhood, the way my parents treated me?

Counselor: Well, it may be. How you think of yourself, how you measure your worth as a person has to do with what you expect of yourself and how you perceive yourself. Your parents may have had certain expectations that you have taken on as your own.

Client: I think that my parents expected a great deal from me. I never could measure up to what they expected.

Counselor: Well, it's true that parents can set up certain patterns for us, but it's equally true that we can change those patterns, if we want.

Client: I feel like I've lived my whole life trying to be the good girl that my parents expected but never being quite satisfied with what I've achieved.

Counselor: It sounds like you have some pretty well-established thought patterns that tell you no matter what you do it's never good enough.

Client: Yes, that's it, exactly.

Counselor: So, now we need to look at some ways of changing that habit of yours of comparing yourself to an unattainable ideal.

Client: I don't know if I can change that. It seems so deeply rooted, beginning in my childhood and all that.

Counselor: Well it's true that the longer you've had a bad habit, the more difficult it is to change it, but that doesn't mean that it's impossible. It will mean more effort on your part, and perhaps a longer period of time in overcoming it.

Client: How do you do that? How do you overcome a rigid upbringing?

Counselor: You can never erase your childhood experiences as such, but what we can work on would be to replace those old, unrealistic expectations with more realistic, adult ones.

Client: I have an awful feeling that I wouldn't measure up even to those.

Counselor: That sounds like a voice from your childhood! Let's look instead at what you have accomplished as an adult, at the situations that you have dealt competently with, at the many stresses in your life that you have learned to cope with.

Client: I guess I've done a few things, but they were all things that were expected of me.

Counselor: Let's leave aside the expectations for now. The fact remains that you have accomplished a great deal: You've developed your talents; you've dealt with demands coming at you from all directions; you've come through some tough times intact.

Client: I know I have done those things, but I still don't feel good about myself.

Counselor: Well, it may be that you've never learned to give yourself credit, or it may be that you're comparing yourself with an unreachable ideal. Which do you think it might be?

Client: I think it's probably both.

Counselor: Well, let's look first at what you expect of yourself. O.K.?

Client: I expect quite a lot.

Transcript of Role Play #3

Client: I'm old and worn out. I'm no longer attractive or good to anybody. I'm not needed by anybody, and most people just regard me as a nuisance.

Counselor: Wow, that's the biggest mouthful of put-myself-down messages that I've heard in a long time! I don't mean that in any sarcastic sense; it's just that all your self-evaluations are so overwhelmingly negative.

Client: I'm just telling you the way that I feel.

Counselor: Right! And you have had legitimate reasons for those feelings. You have been through a lot lately, and it's understandable that you feel tired and worn.

Client: And old.

Counselor: Well, old is a relative term. I feel old, too, sometimes when I see the energy level of younger people and compare that to my own. Going through a trying time can make anybody feel tired and old. I prefer to think of your time of life as midlife or as a crossroads with all kinds of options and possibilities.

Client: I don't see many possibilities. I was never trained or prepared to be anything but a housewife, and now I don't have a house and I'm no longer a wife.

Counselor: Well, let me tell you that I see scores of possibilities for you! The training and maturity that you've gained in your years of being a housewife can stand you in good stead in all kinds of activities.

Client: I can't see any employer wanting to hire me with my background of being a housewife.

Counselor: Well, you'd be surprised how many employer value the maturity and responsibility of middle-aged women. But you don't necessarily have to restrict your options to paid employment. You might want to do things that you enjoy for a while.

Client: I don't like doing things by myself, and I always feel kind of inferior to other women in groups or committees.

Counselor: Well, a lot of women have that same problem of not liking to do things by themselves, and that really cuts down on the options that are open to them. Sometimes, women haven't learned how to enjoy their own company. Or, sometimes, women are afraid of what other people will think when they are seen alone: "She must not be a very nice person because she has no friends," "She is an easy mark," or whatever. Is that what troubles you?

Client: No, I'm more afraid of getting confused, or getting lost, or not knowing what to do next.

Counselor: Oh! That sounds a lot more like the anxiety that anyone experiences when trying out something new. Going out by yourself will be a new experience for you, so it will take some getting used to. It could be kind of exciting, don't you think?

Client: Nerve-wracking would be more like it.

Counselor: Well all of our nerves could use a good wracking every now and then. Shakes them up a bit, saves them from getting stodgy.

Client: It may be good for me, but it will still be difficult.

MEASUREMENT OF BEHAVIOR FEEDBACK

As with the other feminist counseling skills, the amount of behavior feedback used during a client-counselor interchange can be measured. The following scale provides a tool for monitoring levels of skill within segments of counseling interactions. As with the other scales presented in this book, the Behavior Feedback Scale rates transcripts of ten statements by both counselor and client.

Behavior feedback ranges from the lowest level, in which the counselor simply asks questions or makes general statements that may be diagnostic but do not report client behaviors or affect in behavioral terms. At the second level, the counselor is beginning to make behavioral observations at a general level. At the third level, the counselor identifies discrepancies in her observations and provides this feedback to the client. At the fourth level, the discrepancies are identified, with positive attributes being emphasized. At the highest level of behavior feedback, the observations are presented in a manner that encourages client confirmation or disconfirmation of the observations.

The underlying dimensions of the behavior feedback scale are completeness, openness, and positiveness in the counselor's observations of the client.

BEHAVIOR FEEDBACK SCALE

Level I

The counselor asks questions or makes general statements. The counselor does not report any observations of client behavior or reflect the client affect in behavioral terms. Psychodynamic reflection of affect may occur, or diagnostic labels may be applied.

Key Words: *No behavioral observations*

Level II

The counselor makes one response that provides the client with a clear, concise report of observed behavior or behavioral manifestation of affect. The response is in behavioral terms. The response is general.

Key Words: *One general observation*

Level III

The counselor makes two or more behavior feedback responses, one of which at least includes observations of a discrepancy between client statements and counselor observations, or client statements and client behavior, or client self-perceptions and perceptions of ideal self.

Key Words: *Discrepancies reported*

Level IV

Two or more behavior feedback responses are made, with at least one report of observed discrepancies. In addition, two of the behavior feedback responses include references to the client's strengths, abilities, or positive attributes.

Key Words: *Positive qualities emphasized*

Level V

Two or more positive behavior feedback responses, including one report of observed discrepancies, are made, and the counselor asks at least once for the confirmation or rejection of her observations by the client. An opportunity for client disagreement is clearly provided.

Key Words: *Opportunity for disagreement*

CLINICAL APPLICATIONS

The skill of behavior feedback as described can be considered a general, all-purpose counseling skill that is not unique to feminist counseling practice. It is a skill by which the counselor can provide information to the client about herself, "dimples, warts and all," information that will allow the client to take action if she so chooses. The information is clear and concise, easily understood, noninterpretational, and neutral in terminology.

The use of behavior feedback that makes it unique in feminist counseling is its goal and its concordance with feminist beliefs about women's development and behavior change. The goal of behavior feedback in the feminist counseling context is to develop increasingly the egalitarian client-counselor relationship. There are two ways in which behavior feedback accomplishes this. The first is by providing the client with an understanding of the counseling process, by demonstrating to her in clear and simple language what is being observed and reported and indicating why that is significant. By providing the behavior feedback in jargon-free language, the counselor is providing the client with the tools of future self-monitoring.

The second way that behavior feedback facilitates an egalitarian goal is by returning to the client her power in the counseling process, by giving clients the authority to disagree with what the counselor is saying, by verifying her own observations and inferences about behavior.

A more important and controversial aspect of behavior feedback in feminist counseling is its consistency with the feminist philosophy of social determinism in women's behavior. If the primary tenet of the feminist philosophy is that the personal is political, then it follows that behavior change and social action occur in the here and now. Social antecedents of behavior may have occurred in the past, but the remedies lie in the present. A diversionary excursion through the psychosocial relics of our personal past is an interesting luxury that has at best only questionable benefits for changing the present. Childhood influences may constitute a burdensome gunnysack that is still toted around in the present, but that gunnysack can be discarded by picking up lighter and more effective substitutes. A rummaging and resorting of the gunny sack is not always necessary or fruitful.

The philosophy of feminism has been wedded with many different approaches to counseling and therapy, including psychoanalytic approaches and the variants thereof. While the proponents of these psychodynamic approaches would argue that they adhere to the feminist principles of social analysis and egalitarianism in the client-counselor relationship, they nevertheless would not be committed to behavior feedback as a counseling skill. While it is unquestionably true that a valid attempt is being made to incorporate feminist philosophy into established psychodynamic theories, this will of necessity fall short, because the expert counselor or therapist who interprets the client's internal and unknowable self cannot reach an egalitarian relationship with that client. That counselor will always remain distant and essentially removed from her client by the barrier of superiority and expertise.

Although behavior feedback is not a skill unique to feminist counseling, it fits well into the constellation of skills that constitutes the feminist counseling approach. Behavior feedback can be used to bolster the positive evaluation of women, which is the central component of encouraging a woman's reappraisal of the self. By feeding back to a client her strengths and by evaluating them in a positive manner, the counselor can begin to instill a different perspective on the worth of women generally and of the client in particular.

Behavior feedback can also be used effectively with the skills of social analysis and encouragement of total self-development. The behavior feedback can be used to pinpoint those behaviors which are ineffective or detrimental for the client, social analysis can be used to explain how those behaviors were developed and reinforced, and the encouragement of total self-development can show what behaviors are needed and how the client should set about acquiring them. An example of this three-pronged approach might be as follows: A woman exhibits overly compliant behavior by her soft voice, her downcast eyes, and her aversion to conflict. A counselor feeds back these behaviors to the client and indicates what effect they have on others. The counselor uses her social analysis skill to show how these behaviors have been fostered and maintained by female socialization and how these behaviors serve to reinforce women's subordinate status. The counselor then uses her skill of encouraging total development to suggest that more assertive behaviors such as a raised voice, direct eye contact, and assertive self-statements would lead to more effective interpersonal contacts for the client. The counselor might also disclose how such behaviors have benefited her.

Behavior feedback can at times be used in conjunction with the counseling skill of self-disclosure. It can be reassuring to a client who is receiving behavior feedback that might be construed as negative to know that the counselor has also had, and perhaps still has, some experience with that behavior. A counselor who can disclose that she is still intimidated by certain situations and reverts to her passive, feminine self in these situations will be seen as more human and as a more attainable role model than one who appears totally and completely assertive and in control. The behavior feedback from a self-disclosing counselor is likely to be more meaningful, more compassionate, and more sharing than that from one who holds herself more aloof.

Thus, self-disclosure achieves, among other things, an egalitarian counselor-client relationship of the kind created by the use of the behavior feedback skill. This is, therefore, the proper place to describe and analyze the skill of self-disclosure. Like behavior feedback, self-disclosure is not unique to feminist counseling. Nevertheless, it has an important function in the constellation of skills and has a significant impact on counseling goals. In conceptualizing the constellation of skills that constitutes feminist counseling, not only it is important to focus on those skills that are central and unique, that demonstrate the difference of the feminist counseling approach, but it is also important to consider those skills that may be more universal but perhaps are manifest somewhat differently and with a modified purpose in feminist counseling.

Chapter 8

THE SKILL OF SELF-DISCLOSURE

THE SKILL DEFINED

The skill of self-disclosure allows counselors to communicate relevant personal material about themselves to clients. These statements are generally in the form of self-references that are evaluative or descriptive of themselves or are expressions of their personal emotional reactions. The self-disclosures of counselors can vary in immediacy, depth, and frequency. The development of the skill of self-disclosure therefore includes the ability not only to emit self-disclosures but also to gauge their appropriate time, level, and intensity in relation to the clients' needs.

Self-disclosure, like behavior feedback, is not a skill unique to feminist counseling. The counselor's self-disclosure is advocated in many other counseling approaches, primarily because it has been demonstrated that such self-disclosures beget client self-disclosures and foster self-exploration by clients. In feminist counseling, this rationale is acknowledged but is regarded as secondary in relation to the other avowed goals of feminist counseling.

Self-disclosure in counseling is widely espoused in the feminist counseling literature (Krause, 1971; Lerman, 1976; Mander & Rush, 1974; Pyke, 1980; Rawlings & Carter, 1977; Rohrbaugh, 1979; Thomas, 1977). Its purpose has been described in several different ways. Thomas (1977) describes how feminist counselors use self-disclosure to foster a sense of unity or community between women. Women's experiences tend to be fragmented, as each perceives her experiences in isolation and frequently attributes her particular problems and reactions to her own character or shortcomings. A counselor who can disclose her own experiences can help clients to appreciate that many of their problems reflect the common experience of women.

This sense of unity or community between women is also important in the continuing development of a theory of female psychology that takes into account the similarities of the female experience. Psychological theories of human behavior and human development have, to date, really been theories of male behavior and male development. Differences observed in females have been regarded as aberrations, manifestations of an inferior personality type, and deviations from the mainstream of male progression. One of the contributions of feminist thought has been the recognition that an alternate theory of female development is needed, a theory that validates and incorporates the totality of the female experience.

Self-disclosure is one of the vehicles for arriving at such a theory because it establishes the commonalities of the female experience and ascertains what events, feelings, and thoughts are significant for women and how these affect the process of female development. A counselor can indicate to her client that she is concerned about developing a sense of unity among women but also that she is interested in exploring the common experiences for the purpose of theoretical development. In such a way, the process of counseling can be seen as aiding not only the client, who is primarily concerned with her own problems, but also the counselor, who has the secondary concern of developing postulates necessary in forming a theory of female development.

Rohrbaugh (1979) has discussed how the counselor's self-disclosure can serve as a form of modeling for the client, in terms of both content as well as process. It can serve as a model for frank and open communication, a way of expressing one's emotional reactions in a way that is not blaming, negating, or diminishing the behavior of the other. Frequently, women become very proficient at indirect modes of communication. This indirectness is frequently a result of feelings of powerlessness and fear that direct communication will lead to a backlash. A counselor who can disclose her feelings about the client in a nonthreatening, nondiminishing way can, therefore, serve as a model for the client to emulate in her own personal relationships.

The content of the counselor's self-disclosure can provide suggestions or alternative behavioral models that clients may wish to emulate. Feminist counselors do not prescribe behaviors or choices that have been successful for them, but their disclosures of personal experiences and/or behavior can enlarge the scope of options and alternatives for clients to consider. Counselors can report their own variations from traditional female roles, modifications of those roles, and even the satisfaction derived from aspects of traditional roles that have been part of their own experiences. Thereby, clients can be encouraged to reconsider and reevaluate female role behaviors.

Disclosures of negative experiences, too, can be useful in indicating a willingness to take risks with actions that have the potential for failure as well as success. Counselors who can disclose with acceptance and perhaps humor their lapses and blunders can demonstrate that such experiences need not be devastating but rather can serve as sources of information for future trials.

Rohrbaugh (1979) suggests that self-disclosure of personal values and politics can serve to reduce covert bias in counseling. Since counselors clearly influence the kind and direction of change that their clients consider, their disclosure of values regarding women will increase sincerity and trust in the counseling relationship. All counselors have notions of the status of women and of their appropriate roles. By not disclosing these to clients, counselors are likely to influence clients in a particular direction covertly and perhaps unintentionally. Feminist counselors disclose their positions early in the clinical encounter to clarify the direction that the counseling process is likely to take. Clients are thereby provided with clear options about counseling goals and processes.

Pyke (1980) suggests that self-disclosure can serve to attenuate the power differential between counselor and client. Women who ascribe considerable authority to counselors would particularly benefit from such disclosures. The counselor's authority is preserved in traditional counseling approaches by a so-called professional aloofness and noninvolvement. Feminist counseling rejects this superior and aloof stance and instead accepts the notion that counseling can be enriched by making it a reciprocal process in which the human qualities of both counselor and client are open to examination.

Counselors who willingly disclose their own weaknesses, their own foibles, and their own failures as well as successes may initially dismay a client who is searching for perfect and total solutions. In the long run, however, this client is likely to be more ready to accept imperfect and partial solutions, which tend to be the nature of the human condition, when such solutions are modeled by counselors. Although the purpose of counseling is to bring about change, both personal and political, such change is not always imminent or totally realizable. Self-disclosure by a counselor can demonstrate some of the limitations both of counseling and of social action in bringing about desired changes.

Another effect of self-disclosure is egalitarianism in counseling. The counselor who discloses what she thinks and what she feels in many ways becomes as vulnerable as the clients with whom she is working. As the barriers of professional distance and aloofness are lifted, the particular attributes of the counselor become more salient in the counseling situation and open to client evaluation.

Transference and countertransference have been considered to be important psychodynamic counseling processes that are fostered by counselor aloofness and distance. Transference has been said to replicate aspects of the client's personal relationships and to allow for their examination and evaluation in the counseling process. Self-disclosure by counselors mitigates against this transference process in that the counselors are revealed as they are and thereby cease to be those nondescript others who are readily available for transference processes. By engaging in self-disclosure, counselors ensure or at least increase the probability that the clients' feelings about counselors are likely authentic reactions to the counselors' behavior or attitudes and not reflections of their other relationships.

This deliberate negation of the transference process has two important implications. The first is that the counselors accept responsibility for generating emotions and reactions in clients. They recognize that their personal behavior and actions can generate various emotional reactions in clients. These reactions, therefore, need not be interpreted in terms of unconscious mechanisms but can rather be dealt with as reactions to observable precipitating causes. That does not mean that what a counselor says or does never triggers associations for the client or never serves as an echo or reminder of the client's past. However, a trigger or reminder is a very different concept from the process of transference and leads to a very different focus in counseling.

The second implication of discounting transference is that it serves to reemphasize the present orientation and to place the focus on the observable while it minimizes the use of hypothetical psychodynamic postulates. In other words, it reinforces the orientation fostered by the behavior feedback skill, which makes *the present* the primary focus for the counseling encounter.

LEVELS OF SELF-DISCLOSURE

The counselor's self-disclosure to a client can vary in amount, in depth, and in intensity. Its level may depend on the phase of the counseling encounter, on the compatibility between the experience of the client and that of the counselor, on the perceived need of the client, and on the willingness and skill of the counselor in using the self-disclosure skill.

Self-disclosure can range from a complete lack of self-disclosure or completely irrelevant self-disclosure through general or superficial self-disclosures to intimate, emotionally laden disclosures. At the lowest level, counselors actively avoid self-disclosing. Personal questions are turned around, implying that the client is subconsciously seeking some other type of psychodynamic confirmation. At this level, counselors frequently react with responses such as "Why is it so important for you to know about my . . . ?" or "Your asking about my . . . indicates that you have some doubts about your own. . . . " While clients may indeed be asking for reassurance and support, the fact that information is also sought about the counselor is not irrelevant to the counseling process. Such information may be extremely useful in furthering particular counseling goals. At the lowest level of this skill, counselors may also be engaging in self-disclosures that have no relation to the client's life or concerns. Effective self-disclosure must always be related to the client's needs, not the counselor's needs, and it must not be simply a mechanism to fill the counseling hour with interesting conversation.

At the second level, the counselor's disclosures are brief or vague. At this level, counselors are prepared to answer questions or to give brief glimpses of themselves but are basically reluctant to share much about themselves. They may be willing to declare their position on larger questions of philosophy or values but not willing to declare themselves in relation to more personal issues or feelings.

At the third level, counselors freely offer disclosures as they relate to the client's expressed needs, but these disclosures are generally factual or behavioral rather than affective or emotionally charged. Counselors do not give the impression that they would hold back on self-disclosures, but the disclosures offered tend to be lacking in any great emotional investment. Emotional reactions revealed are general rather than particular.

At the fourth level, counselors freely provide information about their own personal ideas, experiences, and feelings when these are relevant to the client's interests and concerns. Counselors at this level are willing to disclose their uniqueness as people and their particular reactions to specific meaningful events in their lives. At the highest, the fifth, level of self-disclosure, counselors reveal intimate information about themselves that might be embarrassing if revealed under different circumstances or if revealed to an outsider. Counselors at this level take considerable personal risks and give the impression of holding nothing back from the client.

Probably the most critical variable in determining the level of self-disclosure that is most appropriate is the phase of the counseling process. A client presenting herself for counseling is initially interested in telling her story, dealing with her distress, and securing some relief. She is not particularly interested in hearing about the counselor. However, some type of informational self-disclosure is important early in the counseling relationship. Counselors who disclose information about their values, their counseling style, and their orientation toward women are presenting information that will enable clients to evaluate the potential of continuing in this counseling relationship. Early self-disclosures can, therefore, be effective when they are informational.

Instrumental types of disclosures, those with a therapeutic or counseling goal, are more effective in the work or action phase of counseling. When a client is actively struggling with a particular problem, trying to resolve some feelings, or considering alternate behaviors, the counselor's self-disclosure may be timely and appropriate. Counselors need to take care, however, that particularly intimate disclosures are offered only when the counseling relationship has developed sufficient depth to allow the client's acceptance of these without embarrassment or discomfort. Too much disclosure at too early a stage can frighten a client, discourage one who is primarily engrossed in her own problem, or serve as an indication to the client that the counselor is not really listening because had she done so she would have appreciated the unique aspects of the client's situation and not strayed with her own experiences.

A counselor's ability of self-disclosure will also depend on the extent of compatibility between her own experience and that of the particular client. Although all women share some experiences and common emotional reactions, the counselor should not minimize the differences between her own experiences and the client's. If the counselor's self-disclosure ignores these differences, it may serve to indicate to the client that the counselor is not sensitive to her unique situation, that the counselor is minimizing the client's problem, or that the counselor is not prepared to acknowledge a lack of expertise or experience with that particular situation.

Client need is an important variable in setting the level of the counselor's self-disclosure. The client who is experiencing intense distress, hopelessness, or fear may be reassured by the counselor's disclosures that indicate that such experiences can be borne and overcome. Clients who are feeling particularly helpless and vulnerable can benefit from the counselor's disclosures that suggest that everyone is periodically subject to such feelings and stresses. Clients who perceive their future as consisting of imperfect alternatives can benefit from the counselor's disclosures that indicate that even such alternatives can lead to satisfying futures.

The level of disclosure is also influenced by the counselor's willingness and ability to disclose her own thoughts and experiences. Effective self-disclosure is a skill that requires considerable confidence on the part of the counselor. Counselors who lack self-assurance tend to be reluctant to disclose themselves for fear of revealing their inadequacies to clients. Most counselors experience some unease with particular clients, but this unease can be disclosed to clients in a beneficial manner when it is presented as behavior feedback that is descriptive and nonjudgmental. Clients can thereby gain an understanding of the effects of their own behavior as well as of the personal reactions of their counselors.

The counselor's willingness to disclose herself also reflects her willingness to take risks, to take the chance of being diminished by her clients, to reveal vulnerabilities or open old wounds, which can be personally painful. It is not likely that a counselor will be equally willing to engage in such behaviors with all clients. Counselors, just like clients, have individual reactions to different individuals, and clearly these enter into the consideration of self-disclosure levels.

Self-disclosure is a potentially powerful skill in the counseling encounter and as such can suffer from inappropriate, overextensive, and indiscriminate use. The use of this skill, like all others, depends on the counselor's sensitivity to what the client is saying, the client's expressed needs, and the stated goals of the counseling encounter.

SUPPORTING RESEARCH

Self-disclosure has been extensively researched. Truax and Carkhuff (1967) studied counselor self-disclosures within the counseling relationship to determine the effects of what they termed "counselor transparency" both on the amount of client self-exploration and on client improvement. Not surprisingly, client self-exploration was positively correlated with positive counseling outcome. As clients became more willing to examine themselves, their chances of benefiting from counseling increased. The willingness of clients for self-exploration was found to be related to self-disclosures by counselors. Counselors who were willing to be transparent or open about themselves with clients were likely to have clients who became equally transparent or willing to engage in self-exploration throughout the course of counseling.

The reciprocal nature of self-disclosure has been well documented. Jourard (1971) in his extensive experimental study of self-disclosure has repeatedly demonstrated that self-disclosure tends to beget self-disclosure. Cozby's (1973) review of the self-disclosure literature indicated a consistent replication of Jourard's findings. In addition to begetting self-disclosure, self-disclosure by counselors has been found to result in more positive and favorable client ratings of the counseling process. Nilsson, Strassberg, and Bannon (1979) found that self-disclosing counselors were liked better and were perceived as warmer, more sensitive, honest, and as possessing a better self-concept than nondisclosing counselors. The authors note, however, that in this study all the disclosures by counselors were positive and similar to the experience of the clients. They suggest that as the counselors' disclosures show more differences from the clients' experience, they become progressively less favorably rated.

The relationship between the amount of self-disclosure and counseling outcome has also been empirically evaluated. These studies, however, have simply looked at one counseling session, usually an initial one, and hence the results are limited to this phase of counseling. Simonson (1976) found that moderate amounts of self-disclosure in the first interview were conducive to the client engaging in self-disclosure, whereas small amounts or excessive amounts discouraged the client's disclosures. Giannandrea and Murphy (1973) likewise found that clients were more likely to return for a subsequent interview when the interviewer had offered moderate amounts of self-disclosure during the first meeting. They also found that such amounts of self-disclosures by counselors resulted in the most positive client evaluations of the session.

The depth or intimacy of the counselor's self-disclosure has also been subject to investigation. Simonson and Bahr (1974) found that counselors who revealed no more than moderately intimate information about themselves in the first few sessios tended to elicit greater client disclosures than those counselors who failed to disclose or those who disclosed intimately. Again, however, it must be noted that this applies to the beginning phase of counseling.

Several studies have investigated the nature of self-disclosures over time and have found that the client's or subject's self-disclosures increase over the time spent with the counselor or experimenter in the study (Cozby, 1973; Strassberg, Anchor, Gabel & Cohen, 1978). Increased disclosures over time were also associated with improvement in the clients and increased liking for the experimenter by subjects. Given these positive effects of self-disclosure over time, it seems likely that increased self-disclosures by counselors over time would also have positive effects.

Reviewers of the research on self-disclosure (Bradmiller, 1978; Cozby, 1973) have generally concluded that divergence in the findings is caused primarily by the complexity of the subject. Variables such as the timing of the disclosure, the degree of intimacy of the disclosure, the expectations of the client regarding appropriate counselor behavior, the level of warmth and nurturance in the relationship, and the counselor's motivation in self-disclosing have all been found to affect the potential benefit of the counselor's self-disclosure to the client.

Self-disclosure in the context of feminist counseling has not been subject to investigation. However, Johnson's (1976) study of feminist therapy clients indicated that one aspect perceived as helpful by the clients was acquiring the knowledge that the counselor had shared a common female experience. Presumably this came about as a result of the counselor's self-disclosure. Whether self-disclosure in feminist counseling actually leads to a more egalitarian client-counselor relationship and whether it promotes the consideration of behaviors modeled by the counselor have not been subject to investigation. An interesting empirical question is to what extent the counselor's self-disclosure facilitates the stated goals of feminist counseling. However, what does seem beyond question is that the general effect of the counselor's self-disclosure is likely to be positive as long as the counselor is sensitive to the client's needs.

CLINICAL EXAMPLES

The following is a synopsis of an actual case in which a couple sought counseling. The husband withdrew after the initial interview, but the wife continued for several subsequent individual sessions. A brief case description is presented and followed by a typical statement of the client. Several different feminist counselors responded to this statement, and their responses are presented as examples of self-disclosure used in a variety of ways. A comment follows each statement by the counselor, discussing her intent.

The Case of Eileen Johnson

Eileen was a thirty-five-year-old married woman with two children who initially presented herself for counseling accompanied by her husband. Eileen's complaint was dissatisfaction with her marriage and her husband's perceived lack of total commitment to their relationship. Herb, the husband, did not share his wife's dissatisfaction. Eileen came from a traditional family background in which her father, a very strong, authoritarian person, had high expectations of his three children. Eileen related that she had high expectations of herself in her current marriage and likewise demanded a considerable amount from her husband. Eileen expected herself to provide gourmet meals daily, to develop her talent as an artist, to coordinate the many activities of her two children, to be totally supportive and responsive to her husband's needs, and to manage her large home with only minimal assistance from her family. Inasmuch as she felt that she was providing maximally for her husband, she expected him to provide maximally for her needs. This was not happening, and she was dismayed and anxious.

Eileen: I want my husband to be my best friend and favorite companion as well as provider and lover. I am interested in everything that he does, and he should likewise be interested in my activities. If you don't share your life together totally, what is the point of being married?

Counselor A: I can think of all kinds of reasons for being married that don't involve total sharing and total involvement. In fact, I'm not at all sure that that kind of total involvement is a good idea in a marriage. I'm happy to be married and share some things with my husband, but I'm equally happy to have my own interests and to be able to do them with my other friends. I would hate to give up those things that I couldn't share with my husband.

Comment: Counselor A is disclosing an aspect of her marriage that is different from Eileen's with the purpose of expanding Eileen's notions of possible marital relationships. The counselor is also disclosing her opinion that Eileen's notion of an ideal marriage may not be a workable one or a desirable one. The counselor is also disclosing that she perceives Eileen's marriage ideal to involve some self-sacrifice that she herself would not be prepared for or happy to consider. The self-disclosure by Counselor A, therefore, is at a general level and has the primary aim of expanding alternatives and considering consequences. The effect of this self-disclosure on increasing the egalitarianism of the client-counselor relationship is likely to be minimal.

Counselor B: The kind of marriage you're describing reminds me of my own ideas about marriage when I was first married. I really resented anything my husband did without me, and I remember making some terrible scenes because he wasn't home punctually from a golf game or he planned to attend some sporting events with his friends without consulting me. It still embarrasses me to think about my ranting and raving! I had to learn to give him some more space in our relationship and to enjoy my own space. Now, I wouldn't give up my own activities for the world! And, you know, our marriage is a lot happier than when I was insisting on total sharing.

Comment: Counselor B is disclosing information about herself at a fairly intimate level, information about herself that reveals her own inadequacies and limitations, but as it relates to events in the past that have been subsequently resolved, the riskiness of the disclosure is curtailed. Counselor B is disclosing an experience that she perceives to be parallel to that of the client. She is indicating that she resolved the situation in a particular way and this may also work for the client. Counselor B is therefore indicating that she was in the same situation as the client but managed to move beyond it. In this way, the counselor is addressing both the egalitarian goals and the alternative expansion goals of self-disclosure.

Counselor C: You know, Eileen, I really enjoy the sessions with you and your husband and with you alone as well. You are both interesting, vital people who are a pleasure to be with. One thing that makes you interesting is your own particular interests and pursuits ... your art, his business. Your husband shares his business concerns with you, but he probably discusses the details of his work with numerous other people. I enjoy hearing you talk about your art; I enjoy your enthusiasm, even though I'm not particularly knowledgeable in that area. I think you would be a tremendous asset to any group that was involved with art or painting. Other people with the same interest as you would probably provide you with much more satisfying feedback than, say, I could or even your husband could.

Comment: Counselor C is disclosing her personal reactions to the client with the purpose of both increasing the client's sense of self-worth and encouraging her total self-development. The counselor's self-disclosures are her present reactions to the client, and they are of a positive nature. She discloses some of her own limitations, but not in a particularly sensitive area. Self-disclosure in this response, therefore, is only of moderate depth and risk level for the counselor even though it relates to the present.

The three examples of the skill of self-disclosure presented above give some indication of the diversity of ways in which the skill can be used to expand the client's perception of alternatives, to model behavior or options by counselors, to reveal personal attributes of the counselors, to diminish the power differential between counselor and client, and to increase the sense of commonality as women between counselor and client.

While none of the counselors engaged in particularly intimate self-disclosures, they revealed enough about themselves in their responses to indicate that they were willing to disclose themselves as it was appropriate to the needs of the client. Intimate disclosures, while they can be very powerful in the counseling relationship, are by nature somewhat infrequent. A counselor who practices intimate self-disclosures indiscriminately is likely to be perceived as superficial or frightening or simply as less competent that one who discloses more appropriately. Self-disclosures, therefore, must always be gauged in relation to the needs of the client and cannot be considered in isolation from the client's statements.

The following role-playing exercises are designed to provide counselors with the opportunity to experiment with a variety of types and levels of self-disclosure. Such experimentation can be used to determine which types of disclosures are most appropriate for particular client situations and which are most compatible with a counselor's particular style. Also, these exercises provide the opportunity for counselors to select for self-disclosure the most salient aspects of their experience. A rambling account of one's experience is likely to be less effective than a succinct statement about the particularly relevant aspect of the experience. Self-disclosures, although always adapted to client needs, also require some skill on the part of the counselor in making the disclosures succinct and relevant to the situation at hand.

ROLE-PLAYING EXERCISES

Role Play #1

Client: I'm always afraid of joining in a conversation, although I very much want to be a part of it.
Counselor: What's the worst possible thing that could happen?
Client: Being made to feel like a complete fool. Has that ever happened to you?
Counselor:

Role Play #2

Client: I've joined a new club but have not been able to pull myself together to go to a meeting.
Counselor:

Role Play #3

Client: I really think that being home with my children is the most important thing at this point in my life. What do you think?
Counselor:

As with the role playing described in earlier chapters, the procedure for the skill of self-disclosure should include the following:

1. Two participants alternating roles
2. Recording of role playing on audio- or videotape
3. Critique of each role play upon completion by participants
4. Review of transcript of corresponding role play
5. Consideration of the modification of role play based on the transcripts
6. Remedial role playing

In the process of analyzing the initial role playing for the skill of self-disclosure, the participants may wish to include the following considerations:

1. Was the self-disclosure of an extent sufficient to provide relevant information to the client without being wordy, digressive, or peripheral to the client's interests?
2. Was the self-disclosure made in response to apparent needs of the client at that point in time?
3. Was the self-disclosure at an appropriate depth or level of intimacy?
4. Did the counselor risk herself at all in making the disclosure?
5. Did the disclosure in any way diminish the power differential between counselor and client? Did it promote an egalitarian relationship?
6. Did the self-disclosure by the counselor promote the sense of commonality between women, particularly between herself and the client?
7. Did the self-disclosure suggest to the client alternatives that had been modeled by the counselor?

The above questions are suggestions or guidelines for the process of examining the role playing. The learner may also compare and judge the role playing by using the transcripts of self-disclosure modeling.

ROLE-PLAYING TRANSCRIPTS

The following transcripts are examples of how experienced feminist counselors enacted the roles presented earlier in this chapter. Again, it should be kept in mind that these transcripts are just examples: They are not prescriptions of how the role-playing situations should be enacted. Self-disclosure is used by each of the counselors in a way that is compatible with her own counseling style and with her perceptions of the needs of the client at that particular time.

A learning counselor can use these transcripts to compare them to her own role playing and to decide if there are aspects of the modeled responses that would enhance her counseling responses.

The suggestion is that the learning counselor should not parrot the responses of the model but rather abstract and/or modify aspects of the modeled responses in a way that is compatible with her own approach and counseling style.

Transcript of Role Play #1

Client: I'm always afraid of joining in a conversation, although I very much want to be part of it.

Counselor: What's the worst possible thing that could happen?

Client: Being made to feel like a complete fool. Has that ever happened to you?

Counselor: Yes, it has, and I've felt a little bad. And then I say to myself that sometimes when you want something you have to take a risk . . . ask questions or make statements that reveal something about myself, and those might not be seen as appropriate.

Client: That's what I'm afraid of . . . that what I say wouldn't be appropriate!

Counselor: But that's the worst that could possibly happen! My experience is that of the hundreds of times that I've joined a conversation, it's only been once or twice that I've felt silly. And I figure that's pretty good odds.

Client: But you probably know what to say. You know how to join in with a group.

Counselor: Well, you know, to join in a conversation you don't have to have anything original to say; you simply want to join in so you say something compatible with the general tenor of the conversation.

Client: Well, I guess that's my problem; I don't know how to judge the tenor of the conversation.

Counselor: You know, I think I've made it sound more complicated than it really is. That's a problem that I have! You know that the most common thing that people talk about is the weather. That's not because it's a burning interest but because it is something that they share with others, and therefore it's a common ground, a common interest that they can share. That's what conversations are—a discussion of something in common.

Client: But I don't want to just talk about the weather.

Counselor: No, of course not. But you do want to talk about something that you have in common with others . . . your interest in politics, in music, or whatever. Women very often talk about their children because that's something they have in common. They can understand each other's problems and celebrate each other's successes.

Client: I find that when people start talking about themselves or their children, they are often bragging, making it sound like they and their families are so great.

Counselor: That may be true in some cases. I find it sometimes helps to tell a story about how things can go wrong, like when I told my son that he could play any sport he wanted as long as it wasn't hockey, and now he is a big league hockey player (and I drive and sit around cold hockey rinks).

Client: I can see how that would work in some situations, but I don't think it would in serious conversations.

Counselor: Well, to tell you the truth, it scares me to join in some conversations, too, but quite often it works to ask questions. Most people enjoy answering questions about themselves or their opinions about a matter. That's something you could do, isn't it?

Client: Yes, I guess so.

Transcript of Role Play #2

Client: I've joined a new club but have not been able to pull myself together to go to a meeting.

Counselor: Well, that's great that you've joined a club. That's a big step.

Client: But I'm afraid to go to the meetings, so it doesn't get me very far.

Counselor: Is there someone you could go with the first time . . . anybody who already belongs to the club, or anybody who might like to join you in going for the first time?

Client: No, the reason I joined was to meet new people, and I don't know anybody else who would want to go to this particular club with me.

Counselor: Well it sounds to me like you'll just have to gather up the courage and take the plunge. You know, just recently I had to meet with a group of influential people who were reviewing a grant proposal I had submitted, and I was scared out of my socks! I almost tripped walking into the room, and my first few sentences were kind of disjointed. But the people were interested in what I had to say, and it got better after a while. I'll bet that you would find the same: People would be interested in you and what you had to say.

Client: But didn't you feel awful when you first walked in? Didn't that make it difficult for you to get going later on?

Counselor: A little, but I was prepared for it to be difficult in the beginning. I knew that I would be nervous and that it would be likely that I would flub the first few things that I had to say. But I find that lots of people are like that and that they are not necessarily judged negatively because of it.

Client: I'm sure that they would all think of me as a dummy after the first few things I said.

Counselor: I think you're being too harsh with yourself. Everybody is entitled to be nervous in new situations, and most people expect and accept that. If you waltzed in all full of poise they might be unnerved and suspicious. Sometimes, if we reveal our weaknesses, others tend to be more protective and supportive. I think that's what happened in my situation.

Client: I suppose . . . I just have to work up the courage to go.

Counselor: Think of it like plunging into a cold lake on a summer's morning.

Client: I don't swim.

Counselor: (laughing) Neither do I.

Transcript of Role Play #3

Client: I really think that being home with my children is the most important thing at this point in my life. What do you think?

Counselor: Well, I can't tell you what is important for you. Is that what you're asking, or did you want my opinion about mothers staying home with their kids generally?

Client: Yes, do you think mothers should stay home?

Counselor: It's hard to make any one statement about all mothers and all kids. I do know that for a lot of women, staying home can be quite difficult because of the lack of stimulation, the sameness of the routine, and so on, but others like it. I have never found it particu-

larly satisfying for me, but that doesn't mean that it can't be for you.
Client: I'm not particularly satisfied, but I think I owe it to my kids.
Counselor: So, are you asking me how much I think mothers should sacrifice themselves or their own interests for their kids?
Client: Uh . . . I guess, something like that.
Counselor: Well I'll tell you that when I am at home and not feeling particularly happy, my kids don't get a very good deal. I tend to be short-tempered and get fatigued from all the routine work. I often give them less than if I'm out of the home part of the day and return to them with a different perspective, but that's because I tend to be dissatisfied at home.
Client: What about being there when they need you? You know, when they come home from school and have something they want to tell you right away?
Counselor: Well, my experience has been that my kids are too busy getting out to play after school to tell me anything. There are other times during the day, at dinner or at bedtime, that they are more likely to talk about their concerns. And if an emergency or something important arises, I can be reached by phone.
Client: So, you're saying that it's not important for mothers to be home?
Counselor: No, I'm saying that it really depends on the mother and on the children involved. For me, it was better to be out rather than to be at home full-time, but that doesn't necessarily mean that the same is true for you.
Client: I feel somewhat the same as you but still feel guilty at the thought of leaving my children.
Counselor: I think mothers are made to feel guilty no matter what they do. If you look after your children all the time you're being overprotective; if you don't look after them all the time you're neglecting them. You have to decide what's best for you and then resolve your feelings around that decision.
Client: But how do you know what is right? I would like to get away from my kids for part of the day, but isn't that just being selfish? I can't always be putting my needs before theirs. After all, they are only children.
Counselor: First of all, there is no absolute right or wrong in

these situations. It depends on what is best for you and for your kids. Every situation is different, and sometimes it takes some trial and error to determine what is right for you. And secondly, thinking about yourself is not being selfish! It's true that your children's needs must be considered, but that doesn't mean that your whole life must be devoted to them. You need to think about yourself, if only to maintain your own mental health.

Client: You make it sound so easy, so logical, but when I try to do something for myself, the kids complain, my husband complains, and I just end up feeling rotten.

Counselor: Well, you may have to learn to put up with a little bit of complaining. Your family has had the luxury of your services; taking that away is liable to generate some complaint. But if you're sure of what you want you can explain it to them and then stand your ground.

Client: That's the trouble! I don't think I can stand my ground. I'm just too soft and mushy inside. I start to feel guilty, and then I just cave in.

Counselor: Well, why don't we work on defining really clearly what you want and need, the rationale for it, and a way of presenting it to your family. If all that is clear ahead of time it may help you to withstand the barrage.

Client: I guess it won't hurt to try.

MEASUREMENT OF SELF-DISCLOSURE

The Self-disclosure Scale measures the extent of, appropriateness of, specificity of, and degree of emotion revealed in self-disclosures by counselors. A counselor's willingness to make herself known to her client at an intimate and personal level is the underlying dimension.

The scale follows the levels of self-disclosure identified earlier in this chapter. It ranges from a lack of self-disclosure or completely irrelevant self-disclosure through general or superficial self-disclosures to intimate, emotionally laden disclosures. At the first level, counselors actively avoid disclosing themselves or do so in a completely inappropriate manner. At the second level, the disclosures are brief or very vague. At the third and fourth levels, self-disclosures are freely offered and are relevant to the client's needs. However, at Level III they are factual in nature or make general reference to emotional reactions, while at Level IV the expressions of emotion are meaningful and specific. At the highest level of self-disclosure, counselors reveal intimate, specific, and immediate emotionally laden information about themselves that displays their vulnerability as individuals.

SELF-DISCLOSURE SCALE

Level I

The counselor actively remains detached from the client and reveals nothing about herself, or if she discloses something about herself it is to meet her own needs exclusively rather than the client's. The counselor changes the focus from herself to the client whenever the client asks personal questions. The only "I" statements that are made are opinions or generalizations that are not personally revealing statements, e.g. "I think most people would feel like that."

Key Words: *Withholds, evades personal questions*

Level II

The counselor, while not always appearing actively to avoid self-disclosure, answers direct questions but does so very briefly. The client, then, only gets to know exactly what she asks about the counselor, and the answers are brief, vague, and/or superficial. The counselor is not afraid to express personal biases or opinions, e.g. "I think women should stay home with their kids," but they are given no immediate personal focus.

Key Words: *Brief, vague, superficial*

Level III

The counselor communicates a readiness to disclose personal information and never gives the impression that she is not willing to disclose more. She may present information about her experience and ideas, but generally these are at a surface level and devoid of much feeling. The client knows only a little about the counselor's emotional reactions to the events in her life, as they are expressed in a general fashion.

Key Words: *Willing with facts, reluctant with feelings*

Level IV

The counselor freely provides information about her own ideas, experiences, and feelings when they are relevant to the client's interests and concerns. The counselor discusses specific personal experiences and feelings and reveals her unique personal reactions to events.

Key Words: *Detailed and meaningful facts and feelings*

Level V

The counselor reveals very intimate and detailed information about her own personality that might be embarrassing under different circumstances or if revealed to an outsider. The counselor gives the impression of holding nothing back. If some of her feelings about the client are negative, the counselor discloses them constructively.

Key Words: *Intimate, risky disclosures*

CLINICAL APPLICATIONS

As already noted, feminist counselors disclose themselves to clients not only to promote client disclosures but also to develop the sense of commonality or unity between women, to eliminate any covert bias in counseling, to diminish the power differential between themselves and clients, and to model alternate options that may be applicable to the client. Self-disclosure therefore becomes more than a simple counseling technique; it is also a statement of a counseling philosophy and feminist values.

Effective counselor self-disclosures are geared to client needs and client readiness. Timing of disclosures must be determined with sensitivity. The counselor discloses only information that the client can presently use to increase her ability to make choices. Feminist counselors are committed to early disclosures of values and philosophy to ensure that clients are fully aware of counseling goals. This commitment, however, does not override the client's needs, concerns, or manifestations of distress. Clients do not always have the opportunity to choose and select counselors, to "shop around" for the most appropriate counselor. Need and/or circumstances may prohibit such shopping, and feminist counselors, just like any other counselors, must attend to the distress of the client. The counselor's self-disclosure must sometimes await the process of attending to the client's immediate needs.

Similarly, in the work or change phase of counseling, a feminist counselor needs to be sensitive to the effects of self-disclosure at any particular moment of time with the particular client. Self-disclosures that are aimed at reducing the distance or power differential between client and counselor may be most appropriate at those moments when the client is feeling that the distance is enormous and divisive. Clients frequently think of their problems as overwhelming and as a reflection of their own personal inadequacies. In this context, counselors are often seen as capable, adequate people, but people who because of their own success may lack the ability even to understand the problem. A disclosure at this juncture can further a counseling process that might otherwise become blocked.

Self-disclosures that are aimed at increasing a sense of female commonality may be most appropriate at times when the client is feeling most alone and bereft with her problems. Again, this sense of isolation and individual responsibility can be diminished by the counselor's self-disclosure.

Disclosures that are aimed at reducing the covert bias in the counseling process are most appropriate at times when counseling goals are being discussed and/or when the client seems to be confused or ambivalent about the goals agreed upon. Although this may occur first early on in the counseling process, it is likely to recur throughout the process. Counseling goals have a way of becoming transformed and modified as they are worked upon. Circumstances change, client perceptions change, and the counselor's awareness of the situation, too, may change: Each of these changes can have an effect on the goals toward which the client is moving. A feminist counselor may have to disclose her own values and philosophical stance repeatedly as the client progresses through her counseling encounter.

The extent or duration of the counselor's self-disclosures is also a variable that must be considered in relation to the client's needs. Effective disclosures are those which communicate the essential information about the counselor in a succinct form. The counselor discloses specific information about herself but not necessarily total information about the circumstances, which may be irrelevant to the point she wants to make. Rambling historical accounts are likely to be perceived as digressions, and the point that is being made is likely to be lost in the verbiage.

Duration of self-disclosures is sometimes influenced by the client as well as the counselor. Clients may find disclosures interesting digressions that shift the focus of counseling away from painful personal material with which they are confronted, or clients may seek such disclosures in an effort to seek premature or instant solutions to their particular difficulties. Counselors, therefore, need to be constantly alert to the purpose of the disclosures, and if the purpose appears contrary to the counseling goals, the counselor can relay this perception to the client through behavior feedback.

The depth or intensity of the counselor's disclosures is a third variable that needs to be considered. To some extent, this will be a function of the life experiences of the counselor. Fabricating experiences to match those of the client is not likely to have beneficial effects. Trust in the counseling relationship can be totally destroyed by evidence of fabrication. Disclosing experiences that are similar but not identical to the client's must also be handled with sensitivity. *Disclosures should never diminish the intensity of the client's experience.* If a counselor chooses to disclose an experience that is similar but less intense, the disclosure should be prefaced with a statement declaring her awareness of that fact.

Positive self-disclosures by counselors generally tend to be perceived by clients as less intense and less powerful than those which reveal some weakness or negative experience. Positive disclosures, which are generally used to promote the client's action in a particular direction, to expand her perception of alternatives, or to increase her evaluation of women, can have the unintended effect of seeming to gloss over difficulties or diminish real problems. Counselors must guard against depicting themselves as Pollyanna, particularly in the context of a feminist analysis that recognizes the real and powerful social constraints that exist.

Self-disclosure by counselors is, therefore, not a counseling skill to be used lightly. It is a skill that to some extent loses its effectiveness with overuse. A counselor who is repeatedly and indiscriminately disclosing herself may be viewed as unconcerned and uninterested in the client. On the other hand, a counselor who makes a particularly intense disclosure, one having experienced circumstances as distressing as those of the client, can significantly change the client's perception of the event. The client can gain hope for the future, strength from a demonstration of human resilience, and a better appreciation of the compassion and ability of others to understand her situation. Many peer counseling approaches are based on the assumption that similarity of a traumatic experience can serve as a bond and means of help for others, and this same principle applies in feminist counseling when those similarities exist.

Self-disclosure has the function, therefore, of aiding the client, but it also has the function of increasing the awareness and knowledge of women's experience. Theories of human development, to date, have largely been theories of male development. Not a great deal of attention has been paid to the transitions or passages of a woman's life or the ways in which women experience these transitions. Feminist counseling has an important contribution to make in aiding women in these transitional phases. Self-disclosures by counselors both within the counseling encounter and outside with their colleagues can contribute to the emerging understanding of women's reality.

Chapter 9

COUNSELING WOMEN IN LIFE TRANSITIONS

The counseling approach described in this book, based as it is on the special skills that form its core, is particularly geared to the needs of contemporary women. It is, however, unlikely that this counseling approach would bring benefit equally to all women in all circumstances. For what kind of women under what circumstances would this feminist approach be most productive?

Evidence regarding the effectiveness of feminist counseling has to date been derived from studies of two types of women. These women have either been young college women or women recently widowed. Young women in the process of establishing a self-identity and life plan, when given a choice, have repeatedly indicated a preference for the feminist counseling approach over more traditional counseling approaches (Johnson, 1976; Marecek, Kravetz & Finn, 1979). These young women have benefited from being helped to understand their own condition in relation to the social status of women.

Women recently widowed have also benefited demonstrably from counseling that incorporated feminist elements. Barrett's (1976) study comparing group counseling approaches for widows demonstrated that a group incorporating consciousness raising or a social analysis was most effective in increasing the sense of self-worth and coping abilities of widows. Clinical case histories and anecdotal data further suggest that women who have recently lost a partner through death, divorce, or separation can derive considerable benefit from a social analysis. Positive evaluation of women can further bolster their self-esteem, while encouraging total development can enhance their coping repertoires. Feminist counseling, which incorporates all these elements, is therefore well suited to these women who are distressed at being newly alone.

175

The success of feminist counseling with young women and women suffering the loss of a partner highlights one particular context of female existence in which such counseling is especially valuable. That is the context of transitional life situations. Young women and women who have lost a partner are all passing through a significant transitional point in their lives. They are giving up previous coping strategies and acquiring new ones. They are discarding old ways of relating to others and developing new ones. Transitions such as these allow particularly for the development of new attitudes and behaviors. Feminist counseling can enlarge women's alternatives at these points and can thus increase the likelihood of their autonomous and independent functioning.

THE NATURE OF FEMALE TRANSITIONS

Transition points in women's lives are influenced not only by their individual needs and capacities but also by the social pressures that reinforce traditional female sex roles. Frequently the strength of either social pressures or individual dynamics is so pervasive that women fail to discover any element of choice during the transition. For example, young women who see marriage as their only option may be responding either to intense social pressure or to intense personal dependence. In either case, no other choices or alternatives are seen as possible. Feminist counseling is very much a matter of presenting and expanding options and choices for women, particularly as they pass through the transitions in their lives. A charting of such transition points could, therefore, provide positive indicators for the use of the feminist counseling approach.

A model of adult development is suggested when considering the charting of transitional points for women. Such models usually consist of a series of progressive hierarchical steps or life crises that are linked to particular age ranges. Generally, both the nature of the steps and the conceptualization of the model have so far been male defined (Erikson, 1964; Levinson, 1978; Valliant, 1977). The unique nature of women's development has largely been ignored, although it is highly unlikely that it follows male patterns in either form or content.

Women's development is unique in several distinctive ways. It is highly influenced by affiliative relationships and by women's high regard for affiliative goals as opposed to achievement goals. It is also severely curtailed by the biological clock, which restricts reproductive capacities to a limited time span. Furthermore, women's development is more highly restricted by environmental and social restraints, which curtail and limit numerous areas of potential personal growth.

Women's development is, therefore, best conceptualized not as a linear or hierarchical process but rather as a spiraling process. A model of a woman's life in society suggested by Peck (1983) depicts the process of her development as a spiral rotating within and influenced by a cylinder representing the demands of her social context. When in the course of the rotation the spiral is subjected to predominantly other-centered demands or social restrictions, the spiral becomes constricted, but in those rotations in which self-attending can flourish, the spiral widens. Furthermore, because environmental and affiliative opportunities can change markedly through this progression, the spiral can move backwards as well as forwards to develop or enlarge capacities earlier neglected. Women's development, therefore, continues through the life span, and both personal characteristics and environmental demands influence its course.

This alternate model of women's development in adult life has important implications when we consider women's psychological distress. If normative female development is not linear or cumulative, then each transition point affords new opportunities for the development of personal strengths, for the utilization and expansion of supportive social networks, and for the overcoming of social pressures and demands that contribute to women's dilemmas.

The unique elements of female development have a considerable impact on successful transitions as well. The female preference for affiliation over achievement is frequently seen as a barrier or handicap to potential development. This is so because the achievement of visible and concrete goals is socially valued, whereas affiliation is regarded as peripheral, part of the process of goal achievement that is unimportant and auxiliary. Generally, there is little recognition that affiliative processes are essential in goal attainment and, further, that affiliation can provide considerable personal satisfaction. Women's attention to affiliation is largely unrecognized except in its absence, when women are soundly condemned. While accepting this low evaluation of affiliative processes and goals, women nevertheless give primary consideration to them in their life transitions.

Women's adult transitions are also marked by their awareness of reproductive functions, which have a greater impact on women's lives than on men's. Fertility can be either a curse or a blessing, depending on women's life situations, and control of reproduction is essential to women's sense of autonomy. Reproductive control, however, in many instances still rests with male-dominated legal and religious structures. Nevertheless, consideration of women's unique capacity for childbirth can significantly affect passages through adult transitions.

Lastly, women's development occurs in a social context in which female accomplishments are accorded only minimal rewards. In that context, social supports are largely lacking, and social expectations are frequently ambiguous or contrary to women's total development and self-fulfillment. Male development, in contrast, is socially supported, with expectations clearly delineated and achievements both socially and personally rewarded. Women, by necessity, must pursue their developmental goals with more vigor and determination in order to travel equivalent distances, and transition points present more difficult choices for many women than for their male peers.

In view of these distinctive characteristics of female development, transition points can be described primarily in terms of relationships or affiliations rather than age-related steps. Environmental as well as relational factors determine the forward or backward spiraling through these transition points as women pursue their total development. A series of possible transition points is as follows:

1. Early womanhood
2. Entry to partnership
3. Entry to motherhood

4. Release from motherhood
5. Dissolution of partnership
6. Late womanhood

These transition points are in no way prescriptive or descriptive of women's optimal development or common to all women. Rather, they reflect points at which women in general have faced difficult choices, points at which they have experienced distress, points at which they have sought guidance in clarifying goals, needs, and ambitions. These transitions are ones that can benefit from feminist counseling skills, skills that enable women to make choices that will maximize their personal growth and development.

The feminist counselor must, therefore, thoroughly understand each transition stage, together with the pressures, dilemmas, and critical choices that distinguish each stage. The present section will attempt to offer such an understanding. A case example in which a woman in transition sought counseling and benefited from the feminist approach will be presented. Role-playing exercises will also be presented to allow counselors to practice their feminist counseling skills in relation to the various transitional stages. Although the case examples and role-playing exercises clearly call for the amalgamation and integration of feminist counseling skills, the particular skills that are most salient to each stage will also be discussed.

EARLY WOMANHOOD

The transition to early womanhood occurs when a woman significantly diminishes her dependence on parental figures and moves toward personal autonomy. This diminution of dependence may be economic (e.g. getting a job), locational (e.g. moving from the parental home), or psychological (e.g. adopting individual value or political positions rather than accepting or reacting to those of parent figures). The rate of progress toward independence is likely to vary in each of these areas and quite likely to be slow when it involves psychological processes.

This goal of independent functioning, while similar for young men and women, is nevertheless differentially reinforced according to gender. Young men are rewarded for independent and autonomous strivings. Young women, in contrast, are rewarded for transferring their dependence from parental figures to a male partner. Achievement and independence are clearly defined for men as primary goals. For women, however, such goals are perceived as conflicting with primary affiliative goals. It is not necessary to explain such conflict as an unconscious "fear of success," as suggested by Horner (1970); rather, it can be seen as a realistic appraisal of the cost of pursuing achievement goals without the necessary social support.

Young women seeking counseling in the process of their transition to womanhood are likely to detail problems related to emancipation from parents as well as conflicting or thwarted affiliative needs. Many young women are still averse to abandoning their search for the elusive male rescuer who will provide the solution to their dilemmas (Dowling, 1981). Social pressures and restrictions discourage many young women from single-mindedly pursuing goals of personal autonomy and individual achievement. Considerable distress is, therefore, frequently experienced by young women as they progress toward adulthood.

Feminist counseling skills can benefit such young women in their conflict resolution. Social analysis can describe clearly the social barriers that restrict their aspirations as well as help them understand their internalized restriction of choices and options. Positive evaluation of women can aid in the recognition that their assets are worthy and deserving of greater social recognition and evaluation. The encouragement of total development can promote the acquisition of needed skills. Self-disclosure by the counselor can provide models of expanded options. Behavior feedback can illuminate for young women their behaviors and attitudes that contribute to the existing problem.

Young women are likely to have experienced some exposure to feminist analysis and to have gained an awareness of the relevance of this analysis to their situation. However, they are more likely to concede that discrimination against women exists generally than to recognize personal discrimination. For example, many young women agree that women's low wages exemplify discrimination but are reluctant to accept that their own occupational choice and position in institutional hierarchies are affected by sex role stereotypes.

Feminist counseling skills can be applied with little reservation to young women experiencing distress in their transition to womanhood. Although the harsh realities of a social analysis may initially be difficult for young women to accept, these will ultimately enable them to plan more strategically and more effectively for their future.

The case example that follows illustrates some typical dilemmas of young women in transition. Although the intervention in the particular case cited below was of relatively short duration, the counselor's feminist analysis had significant impact on the young woman's life planning.

The Case of Francine Rush

Francine sought counseling on the advice of her mother, who was concerned that her twenty-six-year-old daughter was becoming increasingly isolated and increasingly dependent, gaining weight, and becoming slovenly. Francine had recently terminated an eighteen-month relationship with a thirty-five-year-old man. At the end of this relationship, Francine had returned to her parents' home, settled into her old room, and reverted to an adolescent way of functioning. Her parents were concerned not only about Francine's well-being but also about the loss of their own privacy.

While much of Francine's distress related to the rejection by her boyfriend, it became evident that she had handled the termination of the relationship with considerable maturity and evidence of personal strength. When she requested a greater commitment from her boyfriend and he declined, she simply left. She later experienced a pressing need to establish another similar relationship but was dismayed at the lack of suitable persons.

Francine was initially unwilling to consider a more independent, autonomous mode of functioning, as she correctly perceived parental and social expectations that she acquire another male partner to whom to transfer her dependency. Furthermore, having acquiesced to a low achievement standard for young women in her schooling, she found herself in a tedious clerical job that offered little stimulation or prospect for advancement. The development of an independent life-style similar to that of her middle-class parents, therefore, was likely to prove an arduous task.

Counseling with Francine began by highlighting the positives in her past experience: her strength in dealing with the boyfriend, her social skills, which linked her with a large social network, the range and diversity of her interests, which made her an interesting individual and suggested further avenues for development, and her innate intelligence and ability, which she needed an opportunity to exercise.

Social analysis illuminated her pattern of switching dependencies from parents to male partners without considering the possibility of autonomous functioning. Social analysis also explained her tendency to underachieve and her search for fulfillment through affiliative goals. In addition, the ghettoizing of female occupational choices was considered in the social analysis process.

Self-disclosure by the counselor was used to demonstrate the commonality of the female search for affiliation, particularly in transitions to young womanhood. Behavior feedback was used to highlight Francine's strengths, many of which she was only marginally aware of. Encouragement of total development was stressed, as this would enable Francine to exercise her strengths and attain her goal of autonomous functioning.

Francine was encouraged to take stock of her abilities, her interests, and her motivation to pursue further occupational advancement and personal development. At the termination of counseling, she indicated that she had applied for a management position in her company and was considering occupational upgrading as well. She had taken steps to pursue her recreational interests independently, without waiting for friends always to accompany her. She indicated that her parents' concern for her welfare was beginning to become oppressive, and she was looking for her own apartment.

The counseling intervention with Francine was relatively short but was successful because she possessed innate strengths and capacities as well as a supportive family and social network. Young women without these assets are likely to require not only more prolonged intervention but also more concrete help of a financial or occupational nature and more training in social skills.

Role Playing for Early Womanhood

The client statements in the role-playing exercises that follow typify situations of young women seeking counseling. These roles should be enacted in the same way as those presented earlier. The goal here, however, is wider: It is the integration of the five feminist counseling skills into a gestalt that suits the individual counselor's personal style. Counselors are encouraged to experiment with responses and to try different combinations and constellations of feminist counseling skills in order to determine which might be the most effective in particular situations.

Role Play #1

Client: My parents always expect me to take their advice, to accept their suggestions and guidance in everything. Although they seem happy, their way of life doesn't always suit me; yet I don't know what I want for myself.
Counselor:

Role Play #2

Client: My job is rather boring, but I work with a great bunch of girls. I could apply for a supervisory position, but then I couldn't be friends with them . . . and think of all the headaches I'd have! I could use the extra money, though.
Counselor:

ENTRY TO PARTNERSHIP

A major transition point in women's lives is the entry to partnership. Socially sanctioned partnerships have been traditionally regarded as the pinnacle of women's achievements. There has been little recognition that this is in reality a transitional point in women's lives, frequently marked by emotional and familial turmoil. These transitions today can be particularly difficult as newly emerging ideals of egalitarianism contradict male socialization for supremacy and female socialization for submission.

Women's socialization instills in them a perception that their needs, accomplishments, and values are inferior to or less important than those of men. Men, for their part, are taught to expect deference and willing servitude from women. Transitions to more egalitarian partnerships, therefore, are obstructed by the personal and social forces that stand against this new ideal. The power struggles that ensue involve not only male resistance to giving up previous advantages but also women's uncertainty about the legitimacy and desirability of the newly defined egalitarian goals.

Many women entering partnerships have a history of individual pursuits and social advantages that were not too different from those of their male peers. These women, who have so far assumed individual responsibility for their own lives, may find that in partnerships increasing portions of the couple's domestic and social responsibilities are relegated to the woman rather than to the man. Women may express frustration that their partners fail to share equally in domestic activity. At the same time, many women tend to take over, even when their male partners are willing participants. Old and familiar gender-linked expectations may reassert themselves in spite of conscious efforts to overcome them.

Another experience of women entering partnerships is the sense of power differentials in decision making for the couple. Women may express distress at this inequality but remain indecisive about rectifying it because of their own low self-evaluation. Women as well as men tend to believe in superior male economic ability, in greater male rationality, and in the legitimacy of male authority. Women, being ambivalent or unsure of their own abilities, may suffer inequality rather than demand a realignment of authority.

Psychological power differentials are at times accompanied by the exercise of physical power by men against women. Women suffer this abuse frequently because of a lack of confidence to provide for themselves economically, socially, and psychologically. This lack of confidence is reinforced by social stereotypes suggesting that abuse of women is triggered by women, deserved by women, and a fitting punishment for women who fail in their role performance. It is extremely difficult for many abused women to reject the notion of personal responsibility for the abuse and to accept notions of their own adequacy for independent functioning.

Entry to partnership, therefore, frequently involves inequitable distribution of responsibility and power between men and women. These inequalities cannot be overcome by continued female acquiescence and passivity. Women need to be encouraged to value themselves so that they can assert their own needs and demand equal rights. The mere espousal of the ideal of equality in partnership is not enough. Behavior changes must follow, and these changes need to be monitored and reinforced to keep the ideal alive and functioning. Unfortunately, most women entering partnerships lack the skills of assertion, negotiation, and clear and sustained communication that might nurture the ideal of an equitable relationship in a concrete manner. Furthermore, social pressures in the guise of pejorative terminology applied to assertive women and negative attitudes toward independent female partners are frequently exerted to thwart women's efforts in this regard.

Women who seek counseling as they enter or redefine partnerships can benefit from the skills of feminist counseling. Positive evaluation of women is central and crucial to a woman's ability to assert and defend her rights in a partnership. Social analysis can explain the inequality historically built into the institution of marriage and illuminate the social forces that currently continue to reinforce those inequalities. The encouragement of total development can help women to acquire assertive behaviors and negotiating skills that can lead to more equal relationships. Self-disclosure by counselors can serve as modeling or a demonstration of the commonality of women's position in relationships. Counselor feedback can assist women to clarify their ideal images as well as aid in molding new behaviors.

The case example that follows presents a typical example of a young woman considering a partnership. The feminist counseling skills utilized had a significant impact on the young woman's decision regarding the continuance of the relationship.

The Case of Gloria Morris

Gloria, a twenty-eight-year-old nurse, was contemplating marriage with Bob, a twenty-seven-year-old deckhand. They sought premarital counseling as they were experiencing increased conflict and petty bickering as the wedding date approached. They claimed that there was no particular focus for the conflict but rather that it reflected a general dissatisfaction with each other over numerous trivial matters of everyday life.

Gloria was an intelligent young woman who was greatly committed to her profession, fiercely independent, and proud of the fact that she was a self-made woman. Although she came from an upper middle-class background, she had experienced considerable conflict with her parents during adolescence and had left home at age sixteen. Bob, in contrast, came from a lower-class background, from a broken family with a alcoholic mother, and had experienced a number of juvenile incarcerations and a subsequently rather marginal life-style.

In discussing their motivation for marriage, it became clear that what they shared was primarily physical attraction and a rebellious, fiercely independent attitude. Little consideration had been paid to the realities of a future life together, and when practical matters and life goals were discussed, the differences between Gloria and Bob became increasingly evident.

Gloria became increasingly articulate about her expectations of marriage during counseling, expectations that Bob did not feel capable of meeting. He retaliated with disparaging remarks about her previous sexual liaisons, her narcissism, her selfishness, and her lack of compassion. As Gloria become more assertive and confident about declaring her strengths and intention of maintaining her rights, Bob became more hostile, more recalcitrant, and more withdrawn.

Following the second counseling session, Gloria telephoned to state that they had decided not to marry. Gloria had come to realize that her own transition to young womanhood had resulted in a self-definition of failure and that she had been seeking out partners who were similar failures in meeting male standards of success. In the intervening years, Gloria had demonstrated to herself that she was capable and competent professionally, but she had not translated this into a positive social self-image.

Counseling with Gloria and Bob was initially focused on clarifying their expectations of each other. Gloria was encouraged to be explicit about her emerging positive self-evaluation and supported in her notions of androgynous functioning. Social analysis was used to explain the differential expectations that resulted from both gender and class differences in their backgrounds.

Feminist counseling skills were particularly beneficial for Gloria, who needed reinforcement of her positive evaluation of herself as a woman and an individual. The encouragement of total development likewise reinforced her pursuit of androgynous goals, which had served her well in the past. Gloria and Bob both benefited from the social analysis, which helped them to understand their very different expectations. Likewise, they both benefited from behavior feedback, which explicated the attitudinal aspects of their statements, particularly those involving negative messages.

Feminist counseling skills, therefore, are applicable to couples as well as to individual women sorting out the expectations involved in partnerships. Success in modifying disparate expectations depends on both male willingness to forgo traditional power and authority as well as female assertiveness and consistency in making demands and willingness to share the risks and stresses of equality. The goal of feminist counseling in partnerships is to assist partners to maintain their personal autonomy in their individual spheres while working toward equal and shared functioning in their common sphere.

Role Playing for Entry to Partnership

Role Play #1

Client: I find that I'm spending less and less time on my writing and more and more time on doing housework. My husband suggested that I fit in my writing between household chores, but that just doesn't seem to work. I have deadlines to meet, and I'm getting worried.
Counselor:

Role Play #2

Client: My husband continually objects to my friends. He gets mad when I talk on the phone to them; he objects to their visits; he finds fault with all of them. I try to see them when he's not around, but he still complains of my wasting time on them. I find my friends to be a great source of support, but I hate the constant fight with my husband.

Counselor:

ENTRY TO MOTHERHOOD

Recent years have seen the advent of chosen childlessness, chosen deferred motherhood, and motherhood in a variety of relationships bearing little resemblance to the traditional family. Although this increase in conscious choice in the transition to motherhood would suggest increased preparation for motherhood, few women actually find themselves adequately equipped. Many mothers experiencing postpartum distress are well-educated, well-prepared mothers who nevertheless find themselves unable to cope with this transitional phase.

The psychological demands of mothering have increased tremendously during the last century. Child-rearing skill has been turned into so much scientific expertise, and there are so many ready professional advisors, that mothers have all but lost the native abilities and commonsense approach of past generations. Admittedly, women today, themselves raised in small nuclear families, frequently lack previous contact with small children and feel anxious at this gap in their knowledge, but the leap of child-rearing professionals into this gap has resulted in a further erosion of women's self-confidence. The pressure of expert opinion has led to the declaration of impossible expectations and standards of mothering and increased frustration between mother and child instead of relaxed pleasure and joy.

The central issues for women entering motherhood are those of control, competence, and sharing. The loss of control over their lives is a common experience for many women who previously made deliberate and planned choices, including that of becoming a mother, in directing their everyday affairs. No amount of preparation via books or experts can sufficiently alert such women to the incessant and overpowering demands that a new infant can make on their lives. This experience of·being at the mercy of a small, squalling individual with whom reasoning is not possible can be quite distressing and frightening for some women.

Women's sense of personal competence can also suffer severe erosion when they have to deal with the fatigue and repetitive routine of infant care. Positive reinforcements are few, and the results of any child care task are generally short-lived. Little sense of accomplishment accompanies the seemingly endless round of chores. Women who lack social or practical support in child care frequently lose all sense of competence and personal effectiveness.

Entry to motherhood is frequently accompanied by an overwhelming sense of responsibility for the newly arrived infant. Women, particularly, feel responsibility not only for the physical care of the child but also for the psychological and social development of the infant. While shared child care responsibility is increasingly a goal for most couples, this is not an option for women rearing children alone, nor is it, generally speaking, totally attained in the best-intentioned partnerships. Sex role socialization tends to ensure that women attain a greater sensitivity to children's needs as well as a greater sense of responsibility for their well-being. While such socialization experiences can be overcome, social supports and affirmation are not available for men who might seek to assume a primary parenting role. Sex role stereotypes regarding parenting can, therefore, serve to limit choices and options for both men and women in relation to their children.

Entry to motherhood exacts a considerable toll on women's resources. One would expect that women with the benefits of education, life experience, and social stability might be better prepared to cope with this transition, but that does not necessarily follow. Many such women also hold impossibly high expectations of themselves in their new chosen role, and considerable dissatisfaction and distress follow as they perceive themselves functioning inadequately as individuals. The transition to motherhood, perhaps more than any other point, emphasizes the commonality of women and requires an acceptance of personal vulnerabilities and failings.

Women who seek counseling around their transition to mother-hood can benefit from the skills of the feminist counseling approach. Positive evaluation of herself as a woman and mother is central to the coping ability of the individual. Behavior feedback is useful in the examination of ideals that are unattainable and unnecessary. Social analysis is useful in explaining the origins of such ideals and how they serve societal functions at the expense of individual women. Self-disclosure by the counselor can serve to enhance the commonality of the mothering experience, and encouragement of total development can emphasize the individual needs of the woman and decrease the sense of total involvement with the child that many new mothers initially experience.

Feminist counseling, therefore, can be useful in allaying the fears of many women that their negative reactions to this transition bespeak a personal inadequacy and failing in this new role. Societal demands influence the definition of successful mothering, frequently to the detriment of women's individual needs. A feminist analysis offers women a different and more encompassing perspective of this transitional phase.

The Case of Wendy Kane

Wendy was a thirty-year-old professional woman who had chosen to defer child rearing until other life goals had been achieved. However, upon becoming pregnant, Wendy discovered that considerable financial and professional sacrifice would still result from her transition to motherhood. Wendy, intending to breast-feed for as long as possible, took unpaid maternity leave from her job. Her husband, feeling the increased financial stress, worked extra hours and was less available at a time when Wendy needed him most.

After a month at home, Wendy began to feel increasingly depressed, listless, and anxious. A visiting home nurse found her overdressing the baby, overfeeding him, and being overly anxious about the slightest symptom or irregularity. The nurse suggested contact with a postpartum counseling service as well as other child care services.

Wendy was initially reluctant to admit to the presence of personal problems or to her dissatisfaction with her situation. She had deliberately chosen motherhood, and she found it difficult to admit that the transition to domesticity was not as pleasurable or as satisfying as she had anticipated. She found herself socially isolated from her professional peers, understimulated by the home environment, and constantly fatigued by the tedium of the routine. Although her husband was helpful, the total responsibility for parenting was not equally shared. Wendy felt her sense of competence eroding as she struggled to maintain her high standards of housekeeping and child care. She felt that she had abdicated control of her situation to her infant son who now dictated her schedule and plan of activities.

Daily telephone contact was initiated between Wendy and a volunteer from the postpartum counseling service, a woman who had herself previously experienced postpartum distress. This volunteer provided support and encouragement to Wendy.

In addition, Wendy and her husband were seen by a feminist counselor who initially counseled both and later counseled only Wendy. The social analysis used by the counselor enabled Wendy and her husband to understand that domestic responsibilities and the home environment differ considerably from the more clearly defined and structured environment of paid employment. The diffuse and continuous nature of child care and domestic duties requires a more self-defined approach than one based on the external criteria of task accomplishment.

Social analysis was also useful in explaining the overwhelming sense of personal responsibility that Wendy experienced in relation to her child. It was demonstrated to her how the social criteria of motherhood and the social expectations of mothering can lead to a sense of incompetence in the most devoted of mothers.

Positive evaluation of women enabled Wendy to appreciate the intrinsic value of her motherhood role and to enjoy the benefits therein. Mothering, a female activity, was demonstrated to have inherent personal rewards that could be enjoyed. The encouragement of total development was used by the counselor to assist Wendy to explore fully the domestic and motherhood spheres of her current functioning to determine whether these indeed offered sufficient satisfaction and gratification for her personal development.

During counseling with Wendy, the counselor also used self-disclosure to reinforce the supportive messages of the volunteer contact. The message that was repeatedly conveyed was that distress and dismay were not abnormal experiences following childbirth but common reactions experienced by many women. Disclosure by the counselor also served to expand some of Wendy's options as the counselor discussed her own solutions to similar dilemmas.

Wendy decided, after several counseling sessions and much discussion with her husband, to return to work and arrange for day-care for her child. Her husband was supportive and shared in the responsibility of preparing and taking the child to day-care as well as bringing him home and tending to him in the evenings. Wendy initially experienced apprehension and guilt about the day-care arrangement but found that by sharing child care responsibilities and by regaining her sense of competency at work, her attitude and ability to perform effectively at home also improved. Also, by contributing financially to the family income, Wendy decreased the stress on her husband, and he was able to offer more emotional support to Wendy and their child.

The benefits of feminist counseling for Wendy were considerable. Although Wendy did not describe herself as a feminist and on the whole followed traditional ideals of womanhood—indeed, her problems sprang from her attachment to those ideals—feminist analysis allowed her to reconsider some of the restrictive aspects of traditional motherhood while reinforcing the positive and valued aspects of the role. Feminist counseling, with Wendy as with other women, aims always to expand women's options, never to restrict them or to impose different stereotypic notions of appropriate behavior for women.

Entry to motherhood is a major life transition for women who choose to have children. Few women can anticipate the personal demands of this transitional phase. Women with high expectations of themselves in other spheres frequently experience considerable difficulty as these high expectations are transferred to the domestic sphere. Feminist counseling is useful in assisting such women to examine the realities of the situation and to make appropriate choices that reflect their own needs, interests, and abilities rather than social expectations and demands.

Role Playing for Entry to Motherhood

Role Play #1

Client: I feel that I am being a terrible mother. Sometimes I get so frustrated with the baby that I shout at him and feel like shaking him. I know I shouldn't do that, but his constant crying upsets me, and I don't know how to make him stop.
Counselor:

Role Play #2

Client: Sometimes I feel like I'm on a treadmill that is getting harder and harder to push. As I keep trying to do a better job at home with the baby, there just seems to be more that is left undone. I just end up feeling tired and depressed.
Counselor:

RELEASE FROM MOTHERHOOD

Release from motherhood, in contrast to entry to motherhood, can be a gradual and progressive phase that may begin anytime after the arrival of the first child and continue to the maturing of the last. This transition, therefore, varies in time with the subjective experience of a significant life change in any particular woman. This change, which can be defined as the release from motherhood, is the experience of diminished maternal responsibilities with accompanying increases in unrelegated time and energy.

For some women, this transition may go so smoothly as to be almost unnoticed, as alternate activities replace diminishing parental responsibilities. For other women, the transition can be acute and distressing; they experience a diminished sense of purpose in life as children grow up and leave home. This transition has been termed the *empty nest syndrome* and has been associated with the depression of menopause. However, the truth is that release from motherhood need not be a condition to fear, for it offers the potential for considerable personal growth and development at the same time as it offers the reward of seeing one's offspring mature and develop their own autonomy.

The critical issues that mark this transition are a realignment of the women's role networks, consideration of personal options and risks, and reappraisal of sources of personal satisfaction. Transition from motherhood can frequently be a period of major life change for women and may involve a review of personal status and intimate relationships. For many women, this transitional period offers their first opportunity as adults to appraise their life goals. Frequently this reappraisal can involve the totality of personal functioning instead of being limited to only parental roles.

The role realignment that is necessitated by the diminution of the parental role can result in various reactions by women. Some women search out ways in which to extend the parenting role: This is frequently done in volunteer capacities, in which they help their own as well as others' children. This option of volunteering frequently serves as a necessary and useful bridging mechanism for more extensive role realignments later. Other women actively search out and develop new roles for themselves, sometimes beginning activities that were earlier postponed by child rearing. Yet other women may be temporarily thwarted in the process of role realignment, as they perceive only limited options and possibilities for personal development outside the domestic sphere.

Consideration of personal options and risks can be exhilarating for some women while being distressing for others. Personal options clearly vary with such factors as previous education, occupational training, and support of social networks, as well as individual confidence and initiative. In addition, sexual discrimination can constrain women's options, particularly as women reach middle age with only a history of domestic activity marking their background. Risk taking has not been encouraged in them, and pursuing novel life options at this stage can initially induce considerable anxiety. Supportive social networks can greatly influence women's willingness and capacity to engage in risk taking in this transitional phase.

Reappraisal of sources of personal satisfaction frequently accompanies the diminution of parental responsibilities. The rewards of parenting, which may have been considerable during the early, dependent childhood years, are likely to diminish or disappear altogether with conflicts with children over increased autonomy and independence. Women are also likely to find that personal sacrifices and deferment of personal needs "for the sake of the family" are unacknowledged and unappreciated as the family matures. The perceived unavailability of the family as a source of personal satisfaction at this time can frequently trigger a backlash of anger and resentment that focuses on the network of intimate relationships. The realization that personal satisfactions must be sought elsewhere and independently can be difficult for many women.

Release from motherhood thus is a major life transition for women, similar to the much advertised male midlife crisis. It is a period of choices, consideration of options, and lifetime reappraisal for many women. It can be a difficult and painful period as previous choices are reviewed and new courses charted. Alternatively, it can be exciting and exhilarating as new possibilities are explored.

Feminist counseling can be beneficial for women experiencing distress in their release from motherhood. Feminist counseling provides a positive evaluation of women that is necessary to so many women who feel that at this point in their lives they have nothing more to offer. Positive evaluation can assist such women in a more realistic review of their accomplishments and potential for future development. Social analysis can help to explain why women generally feel devalued when maternal responsibilities diminish and can assist in the appraisal of social opportunities and restrictions.

The encouragement of total development is extremely important for women who are experiencing a role realignment and may need to develop aspects of themselves hitherto neglected. The positive aspects of such development may need to be detailed and supported as women pursue unconventional and potentially risky options. Behavior feedback can offer realistic feedback to women as they consider and pursue new options and alternatives. Self-disclosure by counselors may provide modeling of behavioral alternatives or encouragement that positive outcomes are possible.

Release from motherhood, therefore, can be an exciting and positive experience for women. Most women have matured through the experience of motherhood, gained considerable life experience, and developed a greater understanding of themselves and their network of relationships, which can assist the process of reappraisal and review. Unfortunately, the process of review sometimes reveals dissatisfactions and despair about relationships that can no longer be salvaged, and difficult choices about these relationships sometimes accompany the transition from motherhood.

The following case example illustrates how release from motherhood can bring about reappraisal of relationships, resulting in the strengthening of some and dissolution of others.

The Case of Georgina Post

Georgina was a thirty-three-year-old mother of two school-aged children. She initially sought marital counseling for herself and her husband, Ray, because of her increased dissatisfaction with the marriage. Georgina had recently returned to work, and she and Ray both agreed that their conflict had increased markedly since that time.

Georgina described her years at home with the children as personally degrading, stating that her husband had frequently made her feel like a "kept woman" although she had tried constantly and unfailingly to please him. Ray countered that he had always shared household responsibilities and that his infrequent comments on Georgina's slovenly appearance had been misinterpreted and exaggerated.

Georgina had accepted the situation at the time because she felt compelled to maintain a tranquil and pleasant environment at home for the children. She was committed to providing nurturing and support for her children, something she had missed growing up in a large family. Also, in being isolated at home with the children, she lacked any affirmation of the legitimacy of her complaints, especially since her husband continuously told her that she was at fault. She thus kept to herself her many complaints about her husband, storing up the perceived abuses without retort "for the sake of the family."

It was only when she felt released from the responsibilities of motherhood at the advent of her children's schooling that she realized the legitimacy of her complaints and felt the need to air them. As she returned to work and rediscovered a feeling of independence, she began not only to voice her complaints but to remark on them continuously and repeatedly. She stated that this repeated airing of grievances was the only way she could dissipate them, as she felt the need both to reconcile her own feelings and to restructure the marital relationship. Ray, however, countered that he could not live with the barrage of constant negative messages from his wife, and he wanted some immediate decisions made about their relationship.

In counseling, a social analysis was useful with this couple to demonstrate that they were undergoing a not uncommon disruption occasioned by a woman's release from the responsibilities of motherhood and by her increased sense of autonomy and independence. Georgina's self-abnegation during her period of being a dependent mother and homemaker was shown to be typical a response to female socialization. Although Georgina was unfamiliar with the term *feminist*, it was clear that release from motherhood had launched her into a feminist reevaluation of her situation. The anger generated by her perception of previous oppression and submission was all directed toward Ray. Although very willing to assume child care and domestic responsibilities, Ray found the more personal challenges to his authority and masculine power very difficult to endure. His discomfort led him to seek immediate resolution.

The encouragement of total development was applicable to both Georgina and Ray. Georgina was actively developing her assertiveness, but her behavior was sometimes vexingly aggressive. Ray, on the other hand, needed to develop his expressive behaviors and to acknowledge his feelings of dependency on his wife, to modify his masculine necessity to be in control.

Georgina was herself engaged in the process of a positive evaluation of women, building a strong supportive network with her female friends and reevaluating her own strengths. In counseling, this process was interpreted as a positive one, one that could benefit the marital relationship. However, Ray found this difficult to accept, as he perceived it simply as a further erosion of and intrusion upon his authority.

Behavior feedback was important in counseling with this couple, as neither partner was wholly aware of the impact of her or his behavior upon the other. Self-disclosure by the counselor served to demonstrate the commonality of many of the complaints of this couple with other couples involved in role realignment.

Counseling proceeded along a somewhat turbulent course with this couple, as efforts to resolve issues met with frequent setbacks. Georgina found it difficult to relegate her history of perceived oppression to the past, and Ray continued to resent Georgina's increased independence. Ray finally precipitated action by seeking a legal separation. Although both partners expressed some relief at this solution, it was clear that the eventual outcome of the relationship was still in question. Both felt some satisfaction at this temporary hiatus, Georgina having achieved the moratorium she initially requested and Ray having achieved a clear statement on the status of the relationship. Further counseling was declined, as both Georgina and Ray felt the separation had reduced the animosity in the situation to the extent that they could cope satisfactorily.

Feminist counseling skills benefited this couple who, though initially unaware of it, were involved in a restructuring and realignment of their relationship initiated by Georgina's growing feminist consciousness. The social analysis provided in counseling allowed them to see the social ramifications of their conflict as well as to gain an increased understanding of the issues involved. The release from the obligations of motherhood was the precipitating factor in the role realignment, as it allowed Georgina to pursue actively her own development.

Release from motherhood frequently serves as a catalyst to stimulate a period of renewed growth and development in women. Frequently this has an impact on intimate relationships, although not always one as traumatic as in the case described above. It is to be hoped that when women are encouraged and supported in continual personal growth throughout their adult transitions, they will progress through each stage more smoothly and with less disruption of their social networks.

Release from motherhood frequently offers novel and exciting opportunities for women. Acting on these opportunities, however, may involve both risks and costs to the prevailing social equilibrium. Counseling can offer support to women in this transition as well as a realistic appraisal of the situation.

Role Playing for Release from Motherhood

Role Play #1

Client: I find that I have quite a lot of time to myself now that the kids are in school. My husband doesn't want me to go back to work, so I've considered doing volunteer work, but I'm afraid I wouldn't fit in with other volunteer women. What do you think?
Counselor:

Role Play #2

Client: I often find myself questioning my purpose and goal in life, especially when I'm alone at home doing housework. I know that I'm not particularly happy, but I don't know what I should be doing. All I know is that I don't want to be doing the same thing for the next ten or twenty years.
Counselor:

DISSOLUTION OF PARTNERSHIP

Dissolution of partnership is a transitional phase that most commonly occurs through the death of a spouse or through divorce or separation. The age at which a woman experiences this transition can vary from adolescence to old age. Clearly, both the nature of the dissolution and the age at which it occurs will influence the nature of the transition. Emotional reactions, such as grief and anger, are commonly experienced as the task of assuming independent functioning is confronted. Feminist counseling skills are particularly relevant for these women in coping with the emotional and practical problems inherent in resumption of independence.

Dissolution of partnership is undoubtedly most difficult for women who prepared themselves exclusively for marriage and parenthood. Women who are now in their forties or fifties generally grew up with the expectation that marriage was the ultimate adult goal, which would provide security for life. This expectation suddenly turns out to be false when a marriage ends, and that can be a very difficult experience for many women.

Anger, resentment, remorse, and bitterness are among the many negative emotional reactions that can be engendered during this transition. Feelings of loneliness and isolation likewise can accompany the dissolution of a partnership. Accepting such feelings, while not allowing them to become immobilizing, is an important factor in successfully completing this transition.

The primary questions in dissolving a partnership are how to establish independent functioning and how to develop an individual adult identity. Because women have been socialized to regard themselves as the less important and less decisive partner in a relationship, the problem of establishing independent and sustained single functioning can be quite difficult. For some women, the problems seem so immense that they devote themselves entirely to searching out a replacement partner. In some cases, women's inability and unwillingness to stand alone can be a powerful determinant of behavior, one that severely limits options and biases future choices.

The prospect of sustained solitary functioning is frightening for many women, but it offers the possibility of increased personal freedom and self-indulgence. Women who have spent their adult lives subordinating their desires, wishes, and needs to those of others suddenly have the freedom to give full reign to those personal needs. This sense of freedom can be a very positive mobilizing factor in overcoming the negative feelings and constricting factors that accompany this transition.

Dissolution of a partnership frequently involves material restrictions and limitations on women's lives. Single older women frequently find themselves on poverty levels of existence. Socially, a single woman is likely to experience ostracism and find acceptance only among similarly solitary female peers. Vocationally, choices may be limited by both age and gender as well as by personal unwillingness to take on menial or unsatisfying work at this stage in one's life.

The dissolution of partnerships, therefore, presents real, negative emotional reactions and social restrictions. Yet, by releasing a woman from her central commitment, it also offers opportunities and possibilities for positive personal development. Counseling from the feminist perspective can help women to pursue the latter while dealing effectively with the former.

Women who have never entered into lasting partnerships or whose partnerships dissolved in their early years frequently experience a transitional period of this nature at the point in their lives when they realize that future partnerships are increasingly unlikely. Generally, these women have developed successful ways of coping with the practicalities of everyday existence but have retained the longing for a caretaking partner. Giving up this longing and facing the reality of a self-sufficient existence can have the same impact as the dissolution of a partnership that actually existed.

Since feminist counseling has the primary goal of developing female autonomy, it is ideally suited for women struggling with this task during the dissolution of a partnership. A positive evaluation of women is important in counseling women during this transition because a perception of women as strong and capable forms a basis for more effective personal action. Women need to evaluate their assets positively and to see themselves as capable individuals independent from their dissolving partnerships. Developing a separate, adult, personal identity also rests upon the ability to evaluate one's assets and capabilities positively.

Social analysis is useful in assisting women to realize during this transition that their relative passivity, self-denigration, and subservience in partnerships were socially reinforced and fostered. An understanding of the social nature of these traits can replace the sense that these reflect personal failings or inadequacies. In addition, the lower evaluation of the female partner in a relationship can be demonstrated to have a social rather than personal or individual source.

The encouragement of total development aids women during dissolution of partnerships to assume the many and varied responsibilities previously relegated to the partner and to develop those aspects of the self previously neglected in deference to the partner's wishes (or perceptions of the partner's wishes). Behavior feedback can provide ongoing information about the progress of this development while providing an analysis of expectations and notions of ideal functioning. A counselor's self-disclosures, where relevant, may offer hope and promise for the future.

Dissolution of partnerships is never easy and can be particularly painful for women, who tend to invest themselves more heavily in intimate personal relationships. Feminist counseling can help women experiencing such pain and distress both to deal with the pain and to reconstruct a positive and promising individual future.

The Case of Deborah Lee

Deborah was a forty-eight-year-old woman, married for the second time, who was finding the current marriage increasingly intolerable. Her fifty-five-year-old husband, Martin, suffered from a wide variety of physical and psychological problems, demanded constant caretaking and solicitude from her, but gave her little in return. Deborah stated that she was satisfied with her own domestic sphere of functioning but was upset by the tension generated by Martin's complaints and demands.

Deborah had been devastated when her first husband of fifteen years left her, and she had rushed into a second marriage on the basis of little more than physical attraction. With Martin's consuming and pervasive illnesses, the physical and sexual aspects of the marriage dissipated, and the couple found little in the way of common interests or attitudes to hold them together.

Deborah complained bitterly at the onset of counseling about Martin's inability to fulfill her dreams of a second marriage that would salve the hurts of the first. Martin, likewise, blamed Deborah for his ailments, claiming that if she were more caring, more understanding, and more sympathetic, then he would not suffer as much.

Deborah was also bitter about her life circumstances, her inadequate preparation for an independent adulthood, and her economic dependency and lack of vocational training. She felt trapped in an unsatisfying relationship without any viable options.

Counseling with Deborah and Martin initially focused on their individual expectations of the other. Since Deborah was most vocal in expressing her dissatisfactions and unrealized expectations, her options and avenues for personal development within the existing relationship were thoroughly explored. Both positive and negative aspects of the relationship were assesed to determine if the former could be strengthened while the latter could be mitigated.

A positive evaluation of women was used by the counselor to aid Deborah in valuing herself, her abilities, and her accomplishments independent of Martin's affirmation. Social analysis was used to demonstrate the commonality of her situation and to explain the social forces that reinforce female dependency. The encouragement of total development aided Deborah in pursuing her own interests and activities regardless of Martin's participation. Behavior feedback was useful in demonstrating to the couple how their communication pattern was dysfunctional, since each constantly blamed the other, and how this could be remedied. Self-disclosure by the counselor made the couple aware of the stress engendered in families who are coping with illness.

Counseling resulted in considerable changes in the couple's negative communication patterns, instilling in them an appreciation of the positive aspects of the relationship. It also enhanced Deborah's independent functioning and self-evaluation. Martin reported increased satisfaction with the relationship, but Deborah remained ambivalent. Following up the case one month after the termination of counseling, the counselor discovered that the couple had had an amicable separation: Deborah had moved out into her own apartment and was looking for work. Deborah stated that although she and Martin remained in close contact, she had felt the need to be on her own and away from his constant demands. They chose to remain good friends rather than conflictual partners.

Feminist counseling was useful for this couple in demonstrating to them their mutual expectation of being looked after and cared for. Since women are socially expected to assume this caretaking role, it frequently follows that women express the greater dissatisfaction in marital relationships. During counseling with this couple,

Deborah came to recognize the strengths that she had demonstrated in the past and to realize that she was more able to fulfill her own needs than her current partner. As she was not willing to take on her partner's dependency needs and assuage his constant demands, she decided to change the nature of the relationship to what she perceived as a more egalitarian friendship.

Feminist counseling in the dissolution of partnerships has the goal of increasing the autonomy and independent functioning of both partners. While women are initially handicapped by their deficient vocational and economic skills, their superior domestic and social skills frequently enable them ultimately to cope better than their male ex-partners.

Feminist counseling skills can aid women experiencing a dissolution of partnership in using the experience for stimulating growth rather than personal constriction and bitterness.

Role Playing for Dissolution of Partnership

Role Play #1

Client: I've devoted the best years of my life to this marriage; I've taken care of all the household responsibilities and raised the kids almost single-handedly, and now he wants out! If I can't stop him, I'm going to make it as costly and difficult for him to get out of this marriage as I can.
Counselor:

Role Play #2

Client: I'm really angry with my adult children. They know that I'm alone, they say that they will help, but they are never around for more than short periods of time. After all I've done for them, they should be more willing to spend time with me and help me.
Counselor:

LATE WOMANHOOD

The transition to late womanhood can be defined as the period in which a woman confronts her own mortality, faces a shrinking network of peers, and begins to cope with her own decreasing physical and social abilities. This transitional period generally occurs at an advanced age, but women with a life-threatening illness frequently have to deal with many of the same issues. For example, in a study of mastectomy patients, many of whom were in their middle years, Stolar (1982) found that their primary concerns related to the experience of death for themselves and their network of intimate relationships.

Two main tasks of this period can be identified. These are dealing with loss (accepting the possibility of one's own demise) and consolidating personal experiences. These tasks clearly apply to men as well as to women but tend to differ in extent and intensity for women.

Women, who invest heavily in affiliative relationships and who often outlive their male contemporaries, experience repeated and severe losses in their transition to late womanhood. Dealing with these losses can be a draining and taxing experience for women, and their strength in dealing with such losses is frequently quite remarkable.

The consolidation of personal experiences differs for women in that affiliation tends to figure more significantly than achievement. Women confronted with their own mortality frequently report the desire to repair damaged relationships, to strengthen existing relationships, and to extend their network of caring relationships. Consolidation is frequently envisaged as clearly defining one's place in the familial network, a place that will be retained even upon one's demise.

Feminist counseling skills can aid in making the transition to late womanhood a positive experience. The positive evaluation of women can be beneficial in the consolidation of personal experiences, as women can pride themselves in their past achievements and positively value their investment in affiliative relationships. Such positive evaluation can also demonstrate and reinforce the strength of women in coping with their many losses.

A social analysis can help women understand and accept the intense grief that they experience at the loss. Women have often invested the major part of their adult lives in the partnership, so the loss represents not only the physical loss of the partner but also the loss of their emotional investment. Furthermore, the loss frequently entails the loss of a caretaker, a buffer to economic and material concerns and responsibilities.

The encouragement of total development remains an important aspect of counseling with aging women, as even the elderly require feelings of control and influence in their lives. Rodin and Langer (1980), for example, have demonstrated the benefits of personal choices and influence in the lives of the institutionalized elderly.

Feminist counseling with women in late womanhood, therefore, has the goals of legitimizing concerns with relationships and the intensity of grief over personal losses, as well as of consolidating life experiences in relation to one's personal relationships. Furthermore, feminist counseling helps women, even at this late point in their lives, to take action on their own behalf and to pursue their individual goals in the face of the dual passive stereotypes of femininity and age. Feminist counseling, even at this point, aims to promote active participation in key areas of interest and the mobilization of necessary social and personal resources to foster this pursuit. Women need to be actively and maximally in control of their lives for as long as they can.

The following case example is somewhat atypical in that it presents a woman who suffered extraordinary discrimination and oppression in her life but still managed a grand display of strength in the end. While this may not be a truly representative woman, her case does provide a good example of the incredible strength that many women are required to muster during the course of their lives.

The Case of Melody Brown

Melody was a fifty-seven-year-old woman who had been admitted to hospital for chest and stomach pains and then been been transferred to a psychiatric ward following an unilluminating physical examination. Melody had a long history of psychiatric hospitalizations beginning at age thirty-two, when she was diagnosed as schizophrenic, removed to a provincial institution, and housed on a ward for the chronically ill. Her three children were placed in the care of a sister living far away, and her husband divorced her. Melody remained in the institution for many years until the social policy of emptying psychiatric hospitals was implemented, and then she was moved to a community boarding home.

Melody's superior domestic skills and lack of evident symptomatology soon resulted in her finding gainful employment as a domestic to an elderly gentleman, who subsequently married her. Her husband, nevertheless, continued to regard her as a domestic, and as Melody complained of increasing poor health he simply interpreted this as work avoidance and was totally unsympathetic to her complaints. Melody's strength finally failed, and she sought admission to hospital.

Further medical investigations, which continued after the psychiatric transfer, revealed that Melody indeed had a legitimate reason for complaint. She was suffering from inoperable, terminal cancer. Melody accepted this diagnosis calmly, indicating that she had had a premonition of the seriousness of her illness. She also indicated that she had no interest in returning to her husband or to the boarding home but wished to be close to her daughters for her remaining time. She demonstrated realistic expectations for such a reunion, stating that she would not think of living with them or even becoming particularly intimate with them in view of the absence and separation of so many years. Nevertheless, she wanted periodic contact with her children and grandchildren without burdening them unduly.

Melody was assisted in reuniting with her family and in relocating to a boarding home in their vicinity. She died eighteen months later, with her daughters in attendance.

Counseling with Melody was focused on increasing her positive self-evaluation, demonstrating the strengths that had enabled her to deal with prolonged difficulties and to pursue her final objectives. The validity of her aspirations was reinforced, and her valuing of familial relationships was affirmed.

Social analysis was beneficial for Melody in explaining both her perceived powerlessness as a woman and also the stigma of the psychiatric label. Total development was encouraged when she was supported in her active stance in planning her remaining days. Behavior feedback was useful in reiterating her capacity to pursue her goals and in affirming their realistic and valid nature. The counselor disclosed her admiration of Melody in coping with both the immediate situation and her imminent death.

Feminist counseling was beneficial in this situation in that it encouraged an active and positive stance rather than a passive acceptance of fate. It also mobilized and developed latent strengths while assisting in the evaluation and understanding of existing social barriers. Feminist counseling affirmed the importance of affiliative relationships and the necessity of reconciling and consolidating these in life experience. For Melody, it was important to reestablish those relationships so that she could bid them a genuine and significant farewell.

In late womanhood, as in other transitions, feminist counseling is beneficial in helping women to take control and to see themselves positively with the capacity to determine their life course and in providing explanations for perceived failings in terms of social barriers rather than personal deficiencies.

Role Playing for Transition to Late Womanhood

Role Play #1

Client: My life is almost over, and yet there are so many things I have not done. And there was so much time that I wasted.
Counselor:

Role Play #2

Client: I don't want anybody to know about my illness. I don't want the family to know my condition will only get worse. I want everything to go on just as it has. I don't want anything to be different.
Counselor:

This chapter has demonstrated the benefits of feminist counseling for the various transitional points in women's lives. Feminist counseling has an obvious applicability to the problems of contemporary women. Further developments in theory, research, and clinical practice, however, are required to refine both the nature of the approach and its more specific clinical validity.

Chapter 10

DIRECTIONS FOR THE FUTURE

Feminist counseling is a fledgling approach to counseling that offers exciting possibilities for the future even though its evaluation and authentication remain as yet limited. The previous chapters have detailed some of the clinical applications of the feminist counseling approach, some empirical validation of effectiveness, and the substantiating theoretical framework. In each of these areas, it is clear that further development is required to promote the maximal effectiveness of feminist counseling. Therefore, this study concludes by noting the directions to be taken in the future in clinical work, empirical investigation, and theoretical development.

CLINICAL REFINEMENT

Clinically, feminist counseling skills have largely been applied to adult women living relatively conventional life-styles concerned about their intimate relationships with others. While this may be the population of women for whom feminist counseling is most appropriate, little can be said about its applicability to other populations due to lack of pertinent data. There are several client populations for whom feminist counseling skills would seem to be highly appropriate and with whom clinical exploration and possible modifications of the feminist approach might prove fruitful.

Female adolescents are one such population for whom feminist counseling holds great potential benefit. In adolescence, many choices are available that can influence subsequent life directions, and the potential for increasing women's participation in all phases of societal functioning is, at that stage, considerable. Unfortunately, the feminist perspective appears to have had limited impact on this population. Concern with body image and appearance, as evidenced in the increase of eating disorders, tends to overshadow concerns of developing personal competence and autonomy. Equality of opportunity is expected as a right, without the awareness of the many barriers that still restrict such a goal. Ambivalence about self-assertion and total development still prevails among young women who lack the confidence that the pursuit of those goals requires.

Feminist counseling with adolescents requires the development of an innovative approach that, while not thwarting their natural optimism, still encourages them to plan effectively and realistically for the future. Female adolescents, well prepared with knowledge about their capabilities and information about barriers to be overcome, not only can plan effectively for themselves but also can bring about a change in the social milieu for women in the future.

Another population of women for whom feminist counseling could potentially be beneficial is those labeled antisocial or criminal by society. Female criminal activity is on the increase, and violent behavior by women is becoming more common. Sometimes this violence simply reflects women's perceived inability and powerlessness to deal with intolerable situations in any other manner. Women who kill or injure their male abusers frequently describe the process by which they came to see violence as their solitary ultimate option. Feminist analysis of such motivation has been accepted in courts of law as a partial defense of such behavior, and feminist counseling can help women in such situations to reassess their choices and options. Women who resort to criminal behavior, either in passion or by deliberate intent, can be helped through feminist counseling to make a more realistic and positive assessment of their situation and to follow a more rational course of action.

Female criminality is sometimes a result of male control of legal definitions. Prostitution, for example, is defined as criminal because society accepts a masculine moral and legal definition of sexuality, one that gives control to men and subjugates women. While a feminist analysis rejects the defining of such female behavior as immoral or illegal, feminist counseling can be useful in helping women to make other choices and explore other options, if they so desire.

Criminality among both men and women can be a response to perceived personal ineffectiveness in legitimate society. The increase in female criminality may reflect women's growing awareness of their limited impact on the social system. Feminist counseling can offer an alternative in encouraging women to seize the power that is potentially theirs and to work collectively to broaden the total power base available to them.

There are, additionally, a number of particular critical situations peculiar to women that can benefit from a feminist analysis, in which feminist counseling may be most effective in assuaging distress. Rape counseling has been developed from a feminist perspective to diminish the victim's irrational sense of personal responsibility while concurrently increasing her ability to deal with the personal, medical, and legal consequences. Similarly, abortion counseling has evolved from the feminist view that women have the right to control their own bodies and their own destinies. The specific application of feminist counseling skills to these situations needs to be more clearly assessed in clinical practice to determine both the nature of their current usage and their potential for future benefits.

Innovations in clinical practice include not only the expansion and modification of feminist counseling skills but also the clarification and delineation of additional components of the approach. Clinicians need to be aware and critical of their clinical skills, evaluating the previously defined skills and clarifying other skills that have been hitherto unrecognized or unspecified. Feminist counseling will continue to develop as a clinical approach only as long as counselors consciously and deliberately apply it to different populations and different situations while sensitively and professionally monitoring the results. Clinical innovations tend to precede more formal empirical or systematic investigation, and hence the future of any counseling approach largely depends upon the counselors applying their craft.

EMPIRICAL INVESTIGATION

Clinical innovations, while essential to the continued development of a counseling approach, are not sufficient by themselves without the reinforcement of solid empirical evidence of effectiveness. A counselor's subjective impressions of effectiveness and anecdotal data simply cannot sustain the continued development and expansion of a counseling approach, particularly in the current social climate of accountability, clinical responsibility, and fiercely competing solutions to identical problems.

The reluctance of some feminists to ally themselves with empirical investigators is partly due to their differences with traditional counseling goals against which they are often expected to evaluate clinical techniques. While feminism has advocated many broadly based philosophical goals for women, the specification of these goals in terms of operational or measurable quantities has frequently been neglected. This is not entirely a failure, for it arises from a cautious reluctance to prescribe female behavior before a more encompassing understanding of the female experience has been developed. However, in the absence of specified goals, traditional ones will continue to be used. Some tentative efforts at feminist definitions are therefore essential. Furthermore, definitions can only be evaluated in terms of actual practice; hence continual use and evaluation of feminist counseling goals can be instrumental in refining the ultimate definitions.

Feminist counseling requires empirical evaluation of its total effectiveness to establish its place comparatively with other counseling modalities. It is a well-known methodological practice to establish the effectiveness of a counseling mode by comparison with other modes. Evidence to date indicates that feminist counseling has an important place to stake out in the continuum of counseling approaches. It is only through continued evaluation of approaches across situations and populations that the place of feminist counseling can be firmly established.

Lastly, the separate investigation of each of the component parts of the feminist counseling approach needs to proceed without delay, so that a constellation of maximally effective components can be developed. Each counseling skill, acting both alone and in interaction with others, needs to be truly understood and verified to eliminate redundant parts and to strengthen essential ones. Counseling cannot hope to survive as a legitimate remedy to psychological suffering without increased understanding of its mechanisms and essential elements. Feminist counseling can demonstrate that feminist philosophy can be translated into counseling techniques of ultimate benefit to women in distress. This demonstration is most effective when presented with validating empirical evidence.

Empirical validation of feminist counseling in terms of feminist counseling goals, in terms of comparative counseling approaches, and in terms of effective components is necessary for the future of the feminist counseling approach. Feminist counselors may need to heed their own advice of total development and refine their investigative and empirical skills along with their counseling skills.

THEORETICAL DEVELOPMENT

The feminist movement began as a reaction to inequitable treatment of women, grew with the recognition of a common female experience, and will continue to develop as this common experience is translated into theoretical propositions denoting a female world view. Inasmuch as theory about behavior directs remediative efforts such as counseling, a solid theoretical foundation is of primary importance. Feminist theory is evolving and will continue to evolve as long as women are concerned about describing and understanding their own experience.

Surprisingly enough, future developments in theory, research, and practice have been discussed separately in the literature of feminism, as though each should proceed discretely and apart. Nothing could be further from the truth! The development of a counseling approach proceeds most effectively when all three elements are closely and intricately interwoven. Clinical innovations spur on empirical investigation. Theoretical formulations inspire new clinical practices. Empirical investigation leads to modification in both theory and practice. With its focus on integration and total development, feminist counseling is ideally suited to pursue such a developmental course. Feminist counseling has pioneered the integration of the personal with the political and now has the potential for showing the way in integrating all aspects of counseling development.

BIBLIOGRAPHY

Abramowitz, C. V., and Dokecki, P. R.: The politics of clinical judment: Early empirical returns. *Psychological Bulletin, 84*:460, 1977.

Abramowitz, S. I., Abramowitz, C. V., Jackson, C., and Gomes, B.: The politics of clinical judgment: What non-liberal examiners infer about women who do not stifle themselves. *Journal of Consulting and Clinical Psychology, 41*:385, 1973.

Abramowitz, S. I., Howard, B. R., Schwartz, J. M., Yasuna, M., Abramowitz, C. V., and Gomes, B.: Sex bias in psychotherapy: A failure to confirm. *American Journal of Psychiatry, 188*:6, 1976.

Barrett, C. J.: Effectiveness of a widows' group in facilitating change. *Journal of Consulting and Clinical Psychology, 46*:20, 1976.

Bart, Pauline B.: Depression in middle-aged women. In Gornick, V., and Moran, B. K. (Eds.): *Woman in Sexist Society*. New York, Basic Books, 1971.

Bart, Pauline B., and Scully, Diana H.: The politics of hysteria: The case of the wandering womb. In Gomberg, Edith S., and Franks, Violet (Eds.): *Gender and Disordered Behavior: Sex Differences in Psychopathology*. New York, Brunner/Mazel, 1979.

Bergin, Allen E., and Lambert, Michael J.: The evaluation of therapeutic outcomes. In Garfield, Sol L., and Bergin, Allen E. (Eds.): *Handbook of Psychotherapy and Behavior Change: An Empirical Analysis*. 2nd ed. New York, Wiley, 1978.

Bernard, J.: Functions and limitations in counseling and psychotherapy. In Hansen, D. A. (Ed.): *Explorations in Sociology and Counseling*. Boston, Houghton Mifflin, 1969.

Billingsley, D.: Sex bias in psychotherapy: An examination of the effects of client sex, client pathology and therapist sex on treatment planning. *Journal of Consulting and Clinical Psychology, 45*:257, 1977.

Blechman, Elaine, A.: Behavior therapies. In Brodsky, Annette M., and Hare-Mustin, Rachel (Eds.): *Women and Psychotherapy: An Assessment of Research and Practice*. New York, Guilford, 1980.

Bosma, B. J.: Attitudes of women therapists toward clients or a comparative study of feminist therapy. *Smith College Studies in Social Work, 46*:53, 1975.

Bradmiller, Linda L.: Self-disclosure in the helping relationship. *Social Work Research and Abstracts, 14*:28, 1978.

Brien, Lois, and Sheldon, Cynthia: Gestalt therapy and women. In Rawlings, Edna I., and Carter, Dianne K. (Eds.): *Psychotherapy for Women: Treatment toward Equality*. Springfield, Thomas, 1977.

215

Brodsky, Annette M.: The consciousness-raising group as a model for therapy with women. *Psychotherapy: Theory, Research and Practice, 10:*24, 1973.

Broverman, I. K., Broverman, D. M., Clarkson, F. E., Rosenkrantz, P. S., and Vogel, S. R.: Sex role stereotypes and clinical judments and mental health. *Journal of Consulting and Clinical Psychology, 34:*1, 1970.

Brown, C. R., and Hellinger, M. I.: Therapists' atitudes toward women. *Social Work, 20:*266, 1975.

Burlin, Frances-Dee, and Guzzetta, Roberta A.: Existentialism: Toward a theory of psychotherapy for women. *Psychotherapy: Theory, Research and Practice, 14:*262, 1977.

Carkhuff, R. R.: *Helping and Human Relations: A Primer for Lay and Professional Helpers.* New York, Holt, Rinehart and Winston, 1969, vol. II.

Carter, C. A.: Advantages of being a woman therapist. *Psychotherapy: Theory, Research and Practice, 8:*297, 1971.

Chesler, Phyllis.: Marriage and psychotherapy. *The Radical Therapist, 1:*16, 1970.

Collier, Helen B.: *Counseling Women: A Guide for Therapists.* New York, The Free Press, 1982.

Collins, Helen V.: *Counseling Women: A Guide for Therapists.* New York, The Free Press, 1982.

Cozby, Paul C.: Self-disclosure: A literature review. *Psychological Bulletin, 79:*73, 1973.

Danish, S. J., D'Augelli, A. R., and Brock, G. W.: An evaluation of helping skills training: Effects on helpers' verbal responses. *Journal of Counseling Psychology, 23:*259, 1976.

David, Sarah J.: Emotional self-defense groups for women. In Smith, Dorothy E., and David, Sarah J. (Eds.): *Women Look at Psychiatry.* Vancouver, Press Gang, 1975.

David, Sarah J.: Working effectively with women. *Canada's Mental Health, 28:*6, 1980.

Deutsch, C. J., and Gilbert, L. A.: Sex role stereotypes. Effect on perceptions of self and others and on personal adjustment. *Journal of Counseling Psychology, 23:*373, 1976.

Dowling, Colette: *The Cinderella Complex.* New York, Pocket Books, 1981.

Engelhard, P. A., Jones, K. O., and Stiggins, R. J.: Trends in counselor attitude about women's roles. *Journal of Counseling Psychology, 23:*365, 1976.

Erikson, Erik H.: *Childhood and Society.* New York, Norton, 1964.

Feldstein, J. C.: Counselor and client sex-pairing: The effects of counseling problems and counselor sex role orientation. *Journal of Counseling Psychology, 29:*418, 1982.

Fodor, I. E.: Sex role conflict and symptom formation in women: Can behavior therapy help? *Psychotherapy: Theory, Research and Practice, 11:*22, 1974.

Fried, E.: Does woman's new self-concept call for new approaches in group psychotherapy? *International Journal of Group Psychotherapy, 24:*265, 1974.

Friedman, Susan S., Gams, L., Gottlieb, Nancy, and Nesselson, Cindy: *A Woman's Guide to Therapy.* Englewood Cliffs, Prentice-Hall, 1979.

Giannandrea, V., and Murphy, K. C.: Similarity, self-disclosure and return for a second interview. *Journal of Counseling Psychology, 20*:545, 1973.

Gilbert, Lucia A.: Feminist therapy. In Brodsky, Annette M., and Hare-Mustin, Rachel T.: *Women and Psychotherapy.* New York, Guilford, 1980.

Golberg, P. A.: Are women prejudiced against women? *Transaction, 5*:28, 1968.

Gormally, J., Hill, C. E., Otis, M., and Rainey, L.: A microtraining approach to assertion training. *Journal of Counseling Psychology, 22*:299, 1975.

Gottman, John M., and Markman, Howard J.: Experimental design in psychotherapy research. In Garfield, Sol L., and Bergin, Allen E. (Eds.): *Handbook of Psychotherapy and Behavior Change: An Empirical Analysis.* 2nd ed. New York, Wiley, 1978.

Gove, Walter R.: Sex differences in the epidemiology of mental disorder: Evidence and explanations. In Gomer, Edith S., and Franks, Violet (Eds.): *Gender and Disordered Behavior.* New York, Brunner/Mazel, 1979.

Haan, N., and Livson, N.: Sex differences in the eyes of expert personality assessors: Blind spots? *Journal of Personality Assessment, 3*:486, 1973.

Haase, R. F., and DiMattia, D. J.: The application of the microcounseling paradigm to the training of support personnel in counseling. *Counselor Education and Supervision, 10*:16, 1970.

Hansen, L. S., and Rapoza, A. S.: *Career Development and Counseling of Women.* Springfield, Thomas, 1978.

Harris, L. H., and Lucas, M. E.: Sex-role stereotyping. *Social Work, 21*:390, 1976.

Hearn, M.: *Three Modes of Training Counsellors.* Unpublished doctoral dissertaion. University of Western Ontario, 1976.

Hill, C. E.: Sex of client and sex and experience level of counselor. *Journal of Counseling Psychology, 22*:6, 1975.

Holstein, C. M., Goldstein, J. W., and Bem, D. J.: The importance of expressive behavior, sex, and need approval in inducing liking. *Journal of Experimental and Social Psychology, 7*:534, 1971.

Horner, M. S.: Femininity and successful achievement: A basic inconsistency. In Bardwick, J. M., Douvan, E., Horner, M. S., and Guttmann, D. (Eds.): *Feminine Personality and Conflict.* Belmont, California, Brooks/Cole, 1970.

Hurvitz, N.: Psychotherapy as a means of social control. *Journal of Consulting and Clinical Psychology, 40*:232, 1973.

Ivey, Allen E.: *Microcounseling: Innovations in Interviewing Training.* Springfield, Thomas, 1971.

Ivey, Allen E., and Authier, J.: *Microcounseling: Innovations in Interviewing, Counseling, Psychotherapy, and Psychoeducation.* 2nd ed. Springfield, Thomas, 1978.

Ivey, Allen E., and Gluckstern, N.: *Basic Influencing Skills: Participant Manual.* North Amherst, Mictotraining Associates, 1976.

Ivey, Allen E., and Simek-Downing, Lynn: *Counseling and Psychotherapy: Skills, Theories and Practice.* Englewood Cliffs, Prentice-Hall, 1980.

Jakubowski, Patricia Ann: Assertive behavior and clinical problems of women. In Rawlings, Edna I., and Carter, Dianne K.: *Psychotherapy for Women: Treatment toward Equality.* Springfield, Thomas, 1977.

Johnson, M.: An approach to feminist therapy. *Psychotherapy: Theory, Research and Practice, 13:*72, 1976.

Jones, W. H., Chernovetz, M. E., and Hansson, R. O.: The enigma of androgyny: Differential implications for males and females? *Journal of Consulting and Clinical Psychology, 46:*298, 1978.

Jourard, Sidney: *Self-disclosure: An Experimental Analysis of the Transparent Self.* New York, Wiley, 1971.

Kaplan, A. G.: Androgyny as a model of mental health for women: From theory to therapy. In Kaplan, A. G., and Bean, J. P. (Eds.): *Beyond Sex-Role Stereotypes: Readings toward a Psychology of Androgyny.* Boston, Little, Brown, 1977.

Kaplan, A. G., and Yasinski, L.: Psychodynamic perspectives. In Brodsky, A. M., and Hare-Mustin, R. T. (Eds.): *Women and Psychotherapy: An Assessment of Research and Practice.* New York, Guilford, 1980.

Kazdin, Alan E.: The application of operant techniques in treatment, rehabilitation and education. In Garfield, Sol L., and Bergin, Allen E.: *Handbook of Psychotherapy and Behavior Change: An Empirical Analysis.* 2nd ed. New York, Wiley, 1978.

Kelly, J. A., and Worrell, J.: New formulations of sex roles and androgyny: A critical review. *Journal of Consulting and Clinical Psychology, 45:*1101, 1977.

Klein, M. H.: Feminist concepts of therapy outcome. *Psychotherapy: Theory, Research and Practice, 13:*89, 1976.

Krause, C.: the femininity complex and women therapists. *Journal of Marriage and the Family, 33:*476, 1971.

Kravetz, Diane: Consciousness-raising groups and group therapy. Alternative mental health resources for women. *Psychotherapy: Theory, Research and Practice, 13:*66, 1976.

Kravetz, Diane: Consciousness-raising and self-help. In Brodsky, A. M., and Hare-Mustin, R. T. (Eds.): *Women and Psychotherapy: An Assessment of Research and Practice.* New York, Guilford, 1980.

Landfield, A. W., and Nawas, M. M.: Psychotherapeutic improvement as a function of communication and adoption of therapists's values. *Journal of Counseling Psychology, 11:*336, 1964.

Lerman, H.: Some thoughts on cross-gender psychotherapy. *Psychotherapy: Theory, Research and Practice, 15:*248, 1976.

Levine, S. W., Kamin, L. E., and Levine, E. L.: Sexism and psychiatry. *American Journal of Orthopsychiatry, 44:*327, 1974.

Levinson, D. J.: *The Seasons of a Man's Life.* New York, Knopf, 1978.

Lipman-Blumen, J.: How ideology shapes women's lives. *Scientific American, 226:*34, 1972.

Mander, A. V., and Rush, A. K.: *Feminism as Therapy.* New York, Random House, 1974.

Marecek, J., Kravetz, D., and Finn, S.: A comparison of women who enter feminist therapy and women who enter traditional therapy. *Journal of Consulting and Clinical Psychology, 47:*734, 1979.

Milburn, T. W., Bell, N., and Koeski, G. F.: Effect of censure or praise and evaluative dependence on performance of free learning tasks. *Journal of Personality and Social Psychology,* 15:43, 1970.

Mitchell, K., Borzath, J., Truax, C., and Krauft, C.: *Antecedents to Psychotherapeutic Outcome.* Arkansas Rehabilitation Research and Training Center, University of Arkansas, 1973.

Moreland, J. R., Ivey, A. E., and Phillips, J. S.: An evaluation of microcounseling as an interviewer training tool. *Journal of Consulting and Clinical Psychology,* 41:294, 1973. *The New Woman's Survival Sourcebook.* New York, Knopf, 1975.

Nilsson, D. E., Strassberg, D. S., and Bannon, J.: Perceptions of counselor self-disclosure: An analogue study. *Journal of Counseling Psychology,* 26:399, 1979.

Notman, M. T.: Feminine development: changes in psychoanalytic theory. In Nadelson, C. C. and Notman, M. T. (Eds.), *The Woman Patient. Volume 2: Concepts of Femininity and the Life Cycle.* New York, Plenum Press, 1982.

Orlinsky, D. E., and Howard, K. I.: Gender and psychotherapeutic outcome. In Brodsky, A. M., and Hare Mustin, R. T. (Eds.): *Women and Psychotherapy: An Assessment of Research and Practice.* New York, Guilford, 1980.

Parlee, M. B.: The premenstrual syndrome. *Psychological Bulletin,* 80:454, 1973.

Peck, Teresa: *Stage-based Developmental Theories and Women's Lives: Toward a Feminist Model of Women's Adulthood.* Paper presented at the Ninth Annual National Conference on Feminist Psychology, Seattle, 1983.

Penn, Margaret: *T.A. from a Feminist Perspective.* Paper presented at C.A.T.A., Vancouver, 1978.

Persons, R. W., Persons, M. K., and Newmark, I.: Perceived helpful therapists' characteristics, client improvement and sex of therapist and client. *Psychotherapy: Theory, Research and Practice,* 11:63, 1974.

Pietrofessa, J. J., Hoffman, A., Splete, H. H., and Pinto, D. V.: *Counseling: Theory, Research and Practice.* Chicago, Rand McNally, 1978.

Pyke, S. W.: Androgynous therapy. *Canada's Mental Health,* 28:6, 1980.

Rawlings, Edna I., and Carter, Dianne K.: *Psychotherapy for Women: Treatment toward Equality.* Springfield, Thomas, 1977.

Rebecca, M., Hefner, R., and Oleshansky, B.: A model of sex-role transcendence. In Kaplan, A. G., and Bean, J. B. (Eds.): *Beyond Sex-Role Stereotypes: Readings toward a Psychology of Androgyny.* Boston, Little, Brown, 1976.

Riskind, John H.: The clients' sense of personal mastery: Effects of time perspective and self-esteem. In Janis, Irving L. (Ed.): *Counseling on Personal Decisions: Theory and Research on Short-Term Helping Relationships.* New Haven, Yale, 1982.

Rodin, J. and Langer, E.: Aging labels: The decline of control and the fall of self-esteem. *Journal of Social Issues,* 36:12, 1980.

Rogers, C. R.: The necessary and sufficient conditions of therapeutic personality change. *Journal of Consulting Psychology,* 21:95, 1957.

Rohrbaugh, J. B.: *Women: Psychology's Puzzle.* New York, Basic, 1979.

Rosenthal, T., and Bandura, A.: Psychological modeling: Theory and practice. In

Garfield, Sol L., and Bergin, Allen E. (Eds.): *Handbook of Psychotherapy and Behavior Change.* 2nd ed. New York, Wiley, 1978.

Russell, Mary: *Microteaching Feminist Counseling Skills: An Evaluation.* Unpublished doctoral dissertation. Simon Fraser University, Burnaby, B. C., 1982.

Schauble, P. G., and Pierce, R. M.: Client in-therapy behavior: A therapist's guide to progress. *Psychotherapy: Theory, Research and Practice, 11:*229, 1974.

Sherman, J. A.: Therapist attitudes and sex-role stereotyping. In Brodsky, A. M., and Hare-Mustin, R. T. (Eds.): *Women and Psychotherapy: An Assessment of Research and Practice.* New York, Guilford, 1980.

Sherman, J., Koufacos, C., and Kenworthy, J. A.: Therapists: Their attitudes and information about women. *Psychology of Women Quarterly, 2:*299, 1978.

Simon, Leonard J.: The political unconscious of psychology: Clinical psychology and social change. *Professional Psychology, 2:*331, 1970.

Simons, J. A., and Helms, J. E.: Influence of counselor's marital status, sex and age on college and noncollege women's counselor preferences. *Journal of Counseling Psychology, 23:*380, 1976.

Simonson, Norman R.: The impact of therapist disclosure on patient disclosure. *Journal of Counseling Psychology, 23:*3, 1976.

Simonson, Norman R., and Bahr, Susan: Self-disclosure by the professional and paraprofessional therapist. *Journal of Consulting and Clinical Psychology, 43:*359, 1974.

Strassberg, D. S., Anchor, K. N., Gabel, H., and Cohen, B.: Client self-disclosure in short-term psychotherapy. *Psychotherapy: Theory, Research and Practice, 15:*153, 1978.

Stricker, G.: Implications of research for psychotherapeutic treatment of women. *American Psychologist, 32:*14, 1977.

Stolan, G. E.: Coping with mastectomy: Issues for social work. *Health and Social Work, 7:*29, 1982.

Sturdivant, Susan: *Therapy with Women: A Feminist Philosophy of Treatment.* New York, Springer, 1980.

Tanney, M. F. and Birk, J. M.: Women counselors for women clients? A review of the research. In Harmon, L. W., Birk, J. M., Fitzgerald, L. E., and Tanney, M. F. (Eds.), *Counseling Women.* Monterey, Calif., Brooks/Cole Publishing, 1978.

Tennov, D.: *Psychotherapy: The Hazardous Cure.* New York, Anchor, 1976.

Toukamanian, S. G., and Rennie, D. L.: Microcounseling versus human relations training: Relative effectiveness with undergraduate trainees. *Journal of Counseling Psychology, 22:*324, 1975.

Thomas, S. A.: Theory and practice in feminist therapy. *Social Work, 22:*447, 1977.

Truax, C. B., and Carkhuff, R. R.: *Toward Effective Counseling and Psychotherapy: Training and Practice.* Chicago, Aldine, 1967.

Truax, C. B., and Wargo, D. G.: Effects of vicarious therapy pre-training and alternate sessions on outcome in group psychotherapy with outpatients. *Journal of Consulting and Clinical Psychology, 33:*440, 1969.

Valliant, G. E.: *Adaptation to Life.* Boston, Little, Brown, 1977.

Welkowitz, J., Cohen, J., and Ortmeyer, D.: Value system similarity: Investigation of patient-therapist dyads. *Journal of Consulting Psychology, 31:*48, 1966.

INDEX

221